I dedicate this book to my children
Stevens, Sydney, Stacey
To their magnificent Mother Martine
To my Brothers: of any Order
To my Br: and Friends: Constant, Umberto
Gardy, Yves, Sister Cécile
David, Enoch, Emilio, Jacques
To my spiritual father Paul Hubert Jean Michel,
My friend, Brother and Colleague Romy Jean Michel
To a Great Initiate and Emeritus Writer Joël Duez
To Benjamin Jean Simeon for the translation
And to all those who near or far
Contributed to the production of this book.

Contents

THE REIKI
WHAT IS IT

Reiki is a Japanese word that is made up of two syllables:

霊 Rei who refers, to the Sacred side of the life of all that exists, to what is Universal, to what is non-tangible, in simple word to the Cosmic Power. Some will name Him: Creator, First Principle, God, Great Architect of the Universe etc. It is the very essence of life; source.

気 Ki which means Force, Energy, Power, Vibration, Prana, Vital energy, Vibratory bodies. In every living Being this energy exists and this is what animates the Being. Without this Energy, Life flies away. Is it therefore more than necessary to maintain this Power that drives us through a healthy lifestyle. A

Controlled vitality allows the body to be in harmony and to better manage the stresses of daily life. Life is therefore sweeter and more pleasant. The less vital energy there is, the more we are subject to psychic, physical and emotional disturbances.

Just as it is important to have a physical health check-up, it is therefore advisable to have a good idea of your vibration level. It would therefore be a good practice to consult a person qualified in the field of holistic care and this is where Reiki comes into play for us; Naturopathy, Ayurvedic medicine, shamanism among others.

Reiki can be defined as sacred energy, universal power, supreme force. It is not a religion but rather a practice, a healthy use of Cosmic Energy for the well-being of all practitioners and recipients of care. The Reiki practitioner serves as a channel and directs energy, through their harmonized bodies, to the recipient, using their hands, voice through vocalization of mantras and the conscious projection of certain symbols through creative visualization. It is of course in the second degree that the practitioner will begin to use the symbols of Reiki.

Reiki can be practiced by anyone because we have a different degree of healing capacity within us.

However it takes a diligent practice and also a certain preparation associated with an initiation by a Master Teacher Reiki. With universal energy being available for all, how can we say that Reiki is for a select groupof people? All you have to do is put in the necessary effort with a discipline of life linked to practices of meditation, concentration and self-treatment, even tests on plants, animals to begin with. We will surely reach a higher and higher level of vibration by applying the different lessons learned and the wise advice of a Master Teacher who, as a result of your efforts, will continue the process of initiation through the 4 degrees of Reiki.

The Reiki initiation allows to unveil the awakening of consciousness of the Practitioner. In this initiation there is certainly a deep spirituality which pushes the practitioner towards an inner quest, a self-discovery and a price of awareness of his deep connection with the universe. This initiation does not allow you magical powers, extraordinary gifts, but you must first of all open yourself to Cosmic Energy and then use this inexhaustible Energy to use for yourself and or for others. The first degree Shoden brings the Reiki initiate to work on the physical and emotional plans. By this initiation the chakras are purified, aligned and harmonized. Also rooting techniques are taught as well as practices on oneself and on others. The practice on plants and animals is also part of the first degree. This book goes in depth in certain teachings so that the Prospect can have a more complete preparation. Thus, one's initiation to the second degree will be more intense.

The Reiki Initiation takes place over 4 evenings or over 2 days, however, if the future Initiate is part of an initiatory Order such as Freemasonry, Martinism or others and also those practicing Voodoo, the initiation can take place in one day. These initiates have a head start because they are often used to meditation practices, know the chakra system and the flow of Energy, and will understand more quickly the subjects that will be discussed and studied. For example, the Freemason and the Martinist as well as the Vodouisant know the principle of Universal Energy because they are part of an Egregore and the Lodges or Temples where they work are only the reflections of this Universe. They are therefore constantly in connection with the Creative Power during their work.

We can say that Reiki is UNIVERSAL, comes to us from Japan by Master Mikao Usui and can be practiced by everyone because the Cosmic sends out its waves of Unconditional Love continuously and without limit.

HISTORY OF REIKI

It is a discipline that comes from the Far East more precisely from Japan. Founder Mikao Usui, from a high social class family, part of the Samurai, was the secretary of a then minister; which would have allowed him to make various trips around the world. He was born in 1865, in the month of August, on the 15th and passed through on the 9th of March, 1926. He was a Buddhist priest and a master in the art of meditation.

He had to retire for spiritual asceticism accompanied by fasting which earned him the inspiration of Reiki. In the past, the transmission was not codified but was done Orally. The idea of opening a first clinic in Kyoto came from Doctor Hayashi Chujiro who was the first of Mikao Usui's disciples and he used Reiki techniques to treat his patients. Hayashi Chujiro had developed the techniques of laying on of hands using a more Mystical approach to the treatment method.

Hayashi Chujiro initiated some disciples among which Hawayo Takata who brought Reiki to the USA.

She was of Hawaiian origin. She received the Reiki Master degree from Hayashi Chujiro while they were in Hawaii. She trained about twenty Reiki masters, according to some 22. These masters were the propagators of the practice through the initiation of several masters including Westerners.

There are now various Reiki streams, all of which derive from authentic Usui Reiki. We will find the original Usui Reiki, Karuna Reiki, Tibetan Reiki, Gendai Reiki, Violet Flame Reiki... to name just a few. There may be several streams of Reiki suited to various traditions because Reiki is the use of Universal Energy available to all; as we mentioned above. For example, the First Nations peoples of Canada, in their practice respecting nature and in constant harmony with the Universe, do as a sort of Reiki. As well is the Vodouisant which through the use of leaves, perfumes, fumigations and other uses of natural elements also practice a form of Reiki to help their patient to recover from physical, moral and spiritual disorders. Reiki is therefore a practice open to all without limit of social class, color, creed or religion. It is enough to open up and let the flow of the energy of life and universal truth flow through the channels of our body.

So the story goes back to Reiki in Japan and the universe takes it back to the whole earth.

Mikao Usui   Chujiro Hayashi   Hawayo Takata

UNIVERSAL ENERGY

How to achieve a healthy mind in a healthy body? Different traditions designate Vital Energy by the terms: Ki, Chi, Qi, Prana, Chula among Shamans etc. This energy circulates in our physical body by taking paths, meridians, nadis, chakras these different terms are found among others in the sacred texts of Hindus, Chinese etc. This energy is invisible and greatly influences our physical health, our emotional well-being which is very important for our balance in order to be able to lead a healthy life.

This energy is composed of Yin and Yang according to Chinese thought, but we also see this flow of energies in the Tree of Sephiroth (numbers, spheres of energy) through the Cineroth (paths). In the practice of Yoga, energy flows through us, harmonizing the different Chakras, from the top of the head to the tailbone through Ida and Pingala and from the bottom up as well. This is called the rise of the Kundilini.

The Initiatic Orders, Freemasonry, Martinist, Pandragon Druids, to name but a few, know and use Sacred Energy in their ritual as mentioned above. We will go into more detail in the second book: "Reiki level 2 suitable for initiates of various Orders".

When this energy flows freely through us, our physical health is improved. When, on the other hand, imbalances set in, the physical envelope is like a boat sailing uncontrollably in a storm. This envelope sends certain messages to the captain of the vessel through problems such as joint pain, muscle pain, pain in certain organs, headaches, visual disturbances, etc. So it is the boat mechanic's duty to do what is necessary. However, it won't be until the arrival at a port to disembark and find a Mechanic capable of making the necessary repairs to put the ship back in service. This Mechanic is the Reiki practitioner who, by being the channel of Sacred Energy, can help obtain this balance necessary to calm the mind and restore physical health more quickly and of course WITHOUT DISTURBING THE CONSULTATION OF A DOCTOR.

The last point is essential for any good Reiki practitioner as it does not treat illnesses.

Life energy flows all around us and some have the ability to feel or see it. It takes on a different shade of color and also vibrates at certain frequencies which can be felt during a scan of the receiver.

Energy is always available, it is free and is Love. We all have energy at different vibrational levels and this can be easily verified. Relax for a few moments, take 3 deep breaths, breathe slowly as you feel the air entering your lungs. Stay calm, place the palm of one hand about an inch from your forehead. After a few seconds you will feel a gentle heat. You can call it Energy. It is by working with determination and discipline that this warmth will become more noticeable and there will come a time when one will feel the energy of the place over which the palm of the hand is placed. Here you have just had the first experience of Reiki for some.

WHY PRACTICE IT

Reiki will not fix an open fracture, nor restore the psychological health of a person in great depression. Do not hesitate to take flight in the presence of any practitioner believing to be able to replace conventional medicine. Reiki can help a person to experience a situation fully and achieve recovery, or even faster healing.

Reiki therefore helps to recreate this emotional balance which makes it possible to lead a harmonious and healthier life. The manipulation of energies by the practices of Reiki, during the sessions, accentuates the flow of energy which circulates in us. We should not force Reiki sessions on anyone, we can just talk to a person who feels vibrations that would require a few Reiki sessions.

The first application of this practice should be on Self. So by experiencing it, we will already be convinced of its benefits. If you have purchased this book and if you are taking the time to read it, there is a call going on within you to make you aware of this Universal Energy.

To practice Reiki you must above all be a loving, smiling, gentle and calm person. It is necessary to have faith of course, but this faith reinforced by your practices will grow and be strengthened. Then at that moment you can say: I am Reiki, Reiki is Me, Reiki is Us. Because at the end of the day the goal of Reiki is not to convince but to be experienced as a personal experience and subsequently to become a collective affair.

It is certain that Reiki optimizes vital energy, it allows us to control our mental and physical balance. It allows the harmonization of the chakras, resolves certain energy blockages while promoting detoxification of the body. It helps strengthen the immune system and stimulates any healing process. By practicing Reiki, the practitioner and the recipient feel a deep calm, an assured well-being. Finally, its practice is not limited only to humans but to all living organisms: plants and also animals.

Reiki is an experience to be lived in full consciousness. It should be remembered that this practice can be learned by everyone without limitation of sex, color, religion or culture. The journey requires a great deal of dedication, time and above all self-discipline.

Some exercises need to be done often and at regular times. This is for the purpose of mastering the Spirit and giving oneself a discipline of life which undoubtedly leads to greater knowledge and mastery of oneself.

The exercises, which you will find later in this book, will lead you to quickly connect with Cosmic Energy and also to better understand the principles of transmission of energy at a distance. Indeed you will certainly have to make remote energy projections for therapy sessions. It is therefore more than important to understand how the Cosmic Force works and the various vehicles it uses.

Practicing Reiki is not a matter of Great Initiates, but preferably of Great Heart. We will certainly question the benefits of such a practice because it is not yet understood by all and is not the subject of much publicity. The best proof we can give is simply Nothing. I say Nothing because the goal is absolutely not to prove or to demonstrate but to make one feel even a Great inner Peace or a certain Sweetness in our daily life.

The sea has never claimed to be salty, but when you taste seawater you quickly realize that its salinity is real. So it will be up to you to experience Reiki first and then to make practicing it a way of life.

It is important to read the following and fully understand the whole process in order to complete it when you wake up.

Small exercise to do every morning as often as possible:

When I wake up, opening my eyes, I thank the Cosmic which gives me its rays of life. My first breath of Conscious air is made in the softness and control of my organs. I then feel the prana penetrating all my pores, swelling my lungs and spreading in all my organs and above all feeding my energy centers of infinite Love and Joy. Then I can put my feet on the ground, knowing that I am well rooted in this Mother Earth which allows me to stand strong in this world. I feel the loving force of this matrix penetrate me by the bottom rising by the various chakras starting with my Root chakra and moving towards that of the Heart where it will unite with the Cosmic Power that I let penetrate me, starting from the top of my head, through the Crown Chakra, taking the path down to my Heart chakra to finally merge with the Energy of the Earth in the Bridal Room. From this union follows a peaceful distribution to all parts of my body. So at this moment I say that I am Reiki.

This little ritual can therefore be used as your first practice in the morning to connect to the Reiki Energy and start the day on the right foot.

THE REIKI IDEALS OR THE 5 PRINCIPLES

Les idéaux du Reiki

Les cinq idéaux du Reiki

Kyô dakewa	今日だ けは	Juste pour aujourd'hui
Ikaru na	怒るな	Libère-toi de la colère
Shinpai suna	心配す な	Libère-toi de toute préoccupation
Kansha shite	感謝し て	Montre de la gratitude
Gyo wo hageme	ぎょを はげめ	Travaille dur sur toi-même
Hitoni shinsetsuni	人に親 切に	Sois bon envers ton prochain

Just for today

I free myself from all anger

I do not worry

I am full of gratitude

I work hard

I am good to others

Just for today

I live, through this sentence, the present moment, yesterday no longer exists and tomorrow is unknown to me. So we have to focus on the Here and Now. It teaches us to be in the midst of self-procession, in control of our actions, our emotions here and now. The present moment is to be lived consciously. It absolutely involves letting go of anything that is preventing you from growing. Our brain stores so many good and bad things that your intellect is already struggling to sort it out. TV shows, movies, news on the Radio and also comments made by people in your environment, immediate or not, affect your mood and are stored in your subconscious.

The education you receive, the false values that society imposes on you, make it so that you no longer live for yourself but for others. So, it's time to take charge of your real life by consciously and decisively rejecting those things that are not yours.

Second Exercise to complete the first:

In the morning when I look at myself in the mirror, I say to myself, taking a deep breath: I Am here and now, I live in Peace, in Love, in Abundance and I am inspired by true and just thoughts which flow from the Cosmic. I am impervious to all kinds of negative information and I sweat this unconditional Love through my thoughts, words and actions. I am a servant of the Master Plan. I am, I am, I am.

I free myself from all anger

Any moment of anger prevents us from seeing the reality of the situation we are experiencing. We must therefore withdraw into our inner strength, ask for help from the Cosmic, from our inner master, if the situation is beyond us in order to find calm; to calm our mind and thus make the right decisions, take the right actions, etc. Anger is the greatest veil that obstructs the Spirit and prevents us from assuming our responsibilities and doing mea culpa. During these events that push us to get angry, we feel a ball in the solar plexus which is the seat of emotions. We will see, in the section of the chakras, how these centers are extremely related to the various bodies.

When this feeling starts to kick in, if possible, withdraw to a quiet place to breathe and regain control of your emotions. If that is not possible, close your eyes for even a few seconds to refocus. Enter the bedroom of the spouses (your heart) and confidently ask for help from your inner guide who will respond without fail. So, in this surrender of yourself to the power of the Solar Plexus Chakra energy, you will find a gentle, slow peace that will help you deal with the situation with some hindsight. No one is perfect but we are all called upon to improve. There will be moments of anger during which you will lose control. After the storm, it is necessary to analyze: the physiological and, or, psychological signs which precede the explosive moment; the emotions of the moment that made you react and put yourself in this state.

We all have a Master (our deep Self) who, in silence, helps us, influences us and inspires us. By taking the time more often to ask for his support, we will be able to hear his Voice in the silence of our Heart.

I do not worry

Worries never provided a solution to the problems experienced. On the contrary, it brings fear, stress and uncertainty. The concerns will be there to evaluate us, so know that the more you worry about what is bothering you, the more you risk missing out on solutions. It is therefore important to learn to let go so as not to fall into the whirlwind of worries.

The practice of "living in the present moment" will lead us to greater peace of mind. Our worries are the result of a fear of tomorrow. Our brain too often takes control, emphasizing especially situations with unknown results. Our fears, our old wounds fuel these fears and increase the level of daily stress.

Don't let this get you down, take back control by reciting this affirmation over and over again until it becomes manifest truth in your life:

First affirmation exercise:

I don't worry anymore, I'm in the procession of myself,

I am living in the present moment and what must happen will happen for my greater good.

I am the master of my destiny and the Universe always brings me what suits me.

I am full of gratitude

It is wonderful to love life in all its forms. How good it is to listen to the birdsong, the gentle morning breeze on our cheeks, to listen to the waves crashing on the beach. Let us thank the Universe for these free gifts which enhance our daily life and bring us inner peace. Smile free at others it will probably bring comfort to a depressed being.

Before going to bed, analyze your day, relive the wonderful moments that marked this course of the sun from your awakening to this moment when your cozy bed awaits you. You have accomplished great things, if only by having a moment of control over your emotions, over your thoughts, this is a big step in realizing your grip. So congratulate yourself and thank yourself for making great efforts that will continue to enhance your life.

Above all, thank the Universe, the Guides, your inner Master who never cease to inspire you, to nourish you with thoughts of peace, to fill you with their Graces but also thank for the trials which are necessary for your progress towards a greater Awakening of conscience.

Thank you note:

I thank the cosmic for this surge of Energy on the World and on me in particular. I thank those Beings that the Plan provides to my assistance and who inspire me on a daily basis. I thank my inner Master who allows me to make great spiritual progress. I congratulate myself on the efforts made and may it continue for the best of Myself.

I work hard

Be honest with yourself and you will be honest with others. Work is freedom, the freedom to earn a humble living, but above all the freedom to grow up because work is not only about making money but above all it is a constant effort on oneself.

A hundred times on the job, handing over your book is not a vain quote but a motivator that pushes us to constantly improve ourselves. This hard work must be done within the limits of reasonableness. When you are satisfied with the work done, do not question it any more, preferably appreciate the result.

The Reiki practitioner does not postpone the practice until tomorrow but is hard at work and is constantly in harmony with the Universe. Do the exercises so that they become part of your daily routine. This should also apply in your professional activities which will become more pleasant and appreciated.

Assert yourself as an essential worker:

I am a hard worker who does not give in to the task at hand within the limits of my abilities. I work in harmony with others, in joy, peace and love. My work is necessary and I do it with gratitude.

I am good to others

Life is a gift from the Creator, from the One who Is who Was and Who Eternally Will be. We must respect life in all its forms and manifestations. How wonderful it is to see a seed germinate that we have planted, how wonderful will it be not to destroy the tree that the Other has taken care of, watered, nourished by his thoughts, his actions and his love.

Kindness is a source of happiness, peace and is the result of a deep respect for Life in all its forms. When you come to love without expecting to be loved in return, to give without expecting any gratification, when you can reach out to the one who needs it without wishing for the same thing then you can say I am Goodness. This quality comes when your spirituality is high, when you have this certainty that everything is Love, that everything comes from Source and that this Source is Infinite Love.

Another assertiveness practice:

I am this Unconditional Love which circulates in everything and everywhere, which brings into each being the very essence of Life. I am that Goodness that flows from the Creator who created everything out of

Love. I am good at everything and with everything, big and small. I am Love.

Live these Reiki ideals, recite them as often as possible so that they penetrate your inner being and become embedded in your cells to manifest in your daily life. Learn them and vibrate them like mantras by visualizing what they represent. Do this each time you wake up and before you go to sleep, your subconscious will take note of it and your inner self will return the benefits to you.

THE CIRCULATION OF ENERGY

It is said and proven that everything is vibration. Everything, absolutely everything, vibrates at a more or less dense level. It is precisely the vibratory frequency that makes one thing of greater density compared to another. If we could see through matter we would see the cells of the stone which vibrate just like the cells of the tree and so do the cells of the human body.

The life energy, prana, as you want to name it, flows through channels called Nadis, in Ayurvedic medicine. They are also called Ida and Pingala which are of different polarity and intersect at specific points: the chakras. There are, of course, coarse canals like nerves, blood vessels, arteries etc. But our work mostly focuses on the subtle side of it.

These are therefore energy channels, also called meridians, that acupuncturists master well because they are an integral part of the care they administer.

This vital energy is mainly influenced by our state of mind. The more peaceful our minds, the smoother the circulation of energy through the Nadis. Our body is divided from the left side from which Ida circulates the so-called feminine energy and from the right side which is energized by the so-called masculine current that Pingala represents. So then, we have the left Lunar side and the right Solar side and the balance is through our Sushuma spine from which the Kundalini rises; if there is no blockage of one or more chakras. This image can easily be transposed to the tree of the Sephiroth with the two columns J and B balanced by the middle column.

These channels are numerous, they would number 70,000.00. Like the city's drinking water distribution channels, it is often necessary to clean it; by emptying standpipes or replacing pieces of broken pipes or maintaining them in general, in order to provide quality water to residents. The same principle applies for the Nadis. It is often necessary to purify these channels of circulation of energies by practices of breathing, meditation among others. The more regularly the nadis purification practices are done, the higher the level of consciousness.

The Reiki practitioner is therefore a hard worker who constantly self-monitors, self-examines and above all self-purifies. It will help the recipients to channel their energy through the laying on of hands and also through sound advice on how to regain inner peace, as a first step, and also through the practice of controlled breathing and meditation. The role of the practitioner is not to give the recipient a fish but to help him one day be able to sin on his own. Anyone can practice Reiki as mentioned above but often there is a need for a motivator, a trigger, a serious guide to help in this quest for Self-discovery and full Consciousness. If more people practice, then more happiness will be felt on a daily basis and like a gear the latecomers will one day follow the march towards the mastery and knowledge of the Self.

Universal energy uses all possible and imaginable channels to flow and will not be blocked by absolutely Nothing because everything is vibration. This powerful and gentle force of the Universe will then be channeled by the practitioner who will circulate it through his own purified and balanced channels to direct it to the receiver by Laying on of Hands. It penetrates our bodies from all sides. However by an effort of concentration and will related to the creative visualization, the energy will descend from the top of the head to concentrate at the level of the navel and finally bind with the Energy of the Earth which will be mentally directed from the feet to the Ombilicus to form a ball of energy resembling Yin and Yang. This vibration will spread through our arms to penetrate the recipient's bodies and automatically ensure an Energetic balance. This balance will continue on its own after a few therapy sessions.

REIKI AND CHAKRAS

In Sanskrit, the word Chakra means Wheel of Energy. They are invisible, subtle, are not of the physical body but directly related to the subtle body which we will develop later. Traditionally this is often referred to as the 7 major chakras that line up with the spine from the tailbone to above the crown of the head.

Take as an example a radio station that captures waves inaudible to our ears to retransmit the sounds through the speakers. It is therefore necessary to synchronize the emission frequency of the waves in order to allow the station to decode the information and translate it into sound. In the same way, the chakras capture the vibratory waves, the Prana, and make them circulate through the Nadis; in our Subtle bodies. The physical body secretes hormones through the endocrine system as the blood circulates throughout the machine through the blood vessels. These hormones have different functions and are necessary for the proper functioning of the system.

There is a close relationship between the organs and the chakras. A problem with the bladders, for example, may be felt during a scan of the Root Chakra. Sometimes these energy centers are blocked and there can be many causes for this. All the grudges, fears, stress, and our upbringing often contribute to blocking these channels. These are the harmful gangues that lead to physical, psychological and emotional problems.

Muladhara chakra, known as the root chakra, can be the subject of sustained care for any problem with the intestines, colon, joints causing, for example, constipation, hemorrhoids and diarrhea among others. Some skin diseases are also caused by an imbalance of this chakra, but it goes without saying that poor personal hygiene has a lot to do with it. In people with bone, joint, leg, rheumatism and other such problems, we also find an unbalanced root chakra.

It is associated with the Element earth. It is located at the base of the spine between the anus and the reproductive organs, and is associated with the adrenal glands which are found above the kidneys. On the emotional level, any imbalance at this level will be felt by a certain heaviness to be achieved, great fatigue, a feeling of insecurity leading to overwork. We will often lack the strength and determination to do things on a daily basis. People, with a root chakra that is too open or not enough, often suffer from bulimia, passivity and have a tendency to have dark thoughts but can also be dominant, cruel and greedy.

At this stage, this center of force must be harmonized. We will visualize the corresponding image, red in color, at the level of the coccyx, vibrating gently while amplifying. We can also place the stones that correspond to this work on the patient between the legs.

Svadisthana chakra, commonly known as the sacral chakra, sits slightly below the navel always behind the spine. The associated element is water and its color is orange. Our emotions, feelings, anxieties and any lack of creativity are influenced by this chakra. It reflects abnormalities in the reproductive organs, kidneys and also the bladder. The glands concerned are the testes or the ovaries depending on the sex. If the woman has severe pain during her period, then this energy center should be targeted, when checked by the practitioner, and this point will be very hot. Any imbalance at this level will also bring a loss of libido, problems at the sexual level, one can suddenly become very jealous with also a flagrant letting go.

When this chakra is balanced the person has greater self-confidence, is open, passionate and very courteous. Otherwise, people whose chakra is unbalanced are jealous, passive and not very creative. They are also very anxious, angry and do not often trust others.

Manipura chakra, solar plexus chakra, located between the navel and the sternum, relates to the fire element and yellow in color and reflects the state of the pancreas, liver, spleen, nervous system also back pain... People angry, aggressive people often have an imbalance at this level. They feel like they are not at peace, as if they have lost the joy of living. They often have stomach problems, are sometimes depressed, develop diabetes and are also overweight, or even appear skinny. As long as the nights are full of nightmares, when you wake up scared, feel jealousy and aggressiveness, it is time to consult and receive sessions that would help restore inner peace.

When this chakra is balanced, people are more calm, open and spontaneous expressing greater self-confidence. This chakra, in imbalance, is reflected in people by breathing difficulties, stomach ulcers. These people, with this unbalanced chakra, are irritable, sometimes mean and haughty, cannot be assertive and can often panic over nothing.

Anahata chakra, the heart chakra positioned at the level of the middle of the chest, with a green color, therefore at the level of the heart, must be visualized at this place. In connection with the element Air, it stimulates the Thymus, gives indication of the state of the heart, thorax and lungs especially the lower part of these organs. It indicates the quality of blood circulation, blood pressure, respiratory tract, epidermis and helps restore the immune system. Those who have difficulty forgiving, loving with unconditional love, giving selflessly and who often feel exhausted and misunderstood should focus on this chakra in order to harmonize it.

When this chakra is balanced, the person tends to accept Love and also to transmit it. She gives thanks and appreciates the little things in life, she lives in peace. If this chakra is not balanced then signs of madness of grandeur, of egocentricity, of a need to overspend appear. The person then shows signs of loneliness, paranoia and falls into an exaggerated withdrawal into oneself.

Vishudda chakra, famous throat chakra, pale blue color, found in the middle of the neck, refers to the Ether and the thyroid glands and the closest organs: throat, neck, jaws, arms, voice of course . When this chakra is balanced we have an ease in expressing ourselves. We then feel inspired with great self-confidence. Independent, upright, and true people have this chakra that vibrates without blocking. Anyone who feels an inability to express themselves clearly, who lacks inspiration, who is inclined to lie can contact a Reiki practitioner for a rebalancing of this chakra.

Often people with this unbalanced chakra will experience neck pain, neck pain, often experience pain in the throat. It happens that sensations of discomfort in the jaws, vocal cords are also felt. Emotionally, these people will be inclined to speak inconsistently, they will also stutter.

Ajna chakra, frontal chakra which vibrates at the level of the forehead precisely between the two eyebrows, the color associated with it is royal blue and it is related to the true light, the inner light and to the epiphysis. Any disorder of the eye especially the left, difficulty concentrating, headaches, brain diseases, vision problems are related. When we feel these kinds of disturbances we must proceed to harmonize this chakra.

People who have this well balanced chakra meditate more easily, have great intuition, and have a clearer perception of the Divine than others. These people are often detached from the material world, calm in nature and with great serenity. They have very pronounced capacities of telepathy, clear hearing and even clairvoyance. However people with this unbalanced chakra will often be confused, age faster, have hearing problems and also vision problems.

Sahasrara chakra, purple crown chakra, Kether, the crown of the tree of life is the illustrious chosen one of 7. It is located at the top of the skull and vibrates with the element Thought, the Spirit and is associated with the gland pineal and governs the central brain therefore the right hemisphere. Any imbalance of this chakra will be felt in the right eye with problems of great weaknesses in the immune system, major nervous or even psychic disorders, difficulty in memorizing. If we have a drive towards spirituality, a desire to express great wisdom, then the call is there for an awakening of this chakra.

You meet people with high thoughts, expressing great wisdom, inspiring deep respect, so it goes without saying that this chakra in these people is vibrating harmoniously. These people will often be in contemplation, with great generosity and they often give of themselves. On the other hand, those who have this weak chakra will have repeated headaches, chronic diseases and will present brain tumors.

CHAKRA 7		OM	SAHASRARA
CHAKRA 6		OM	AJNA
CHAKRA 5		HAM	VISUDDHA
CHAKRA 4		YAM	ANAHATA
CHAKRA 3		RAM	MANIPURA
CHAKRA 2		VAM	SVADHISTHANA
CHAKRA 1		LAM	MULADHARA

A great Gnostic Initiate, Samael Aun Weor, correlates with the Seven Churches of Revelation (see the Bible) which function during the rise of the Kundalini. Certainly this refers to the practice of Sexual magic which allows the meteoric rise of the Kundalini not without danger because it takes a great mastery and understanding and studies on sexual magic. It also becomes a way of proceeding with the harmonization of the chakras.

Here we make a comparison of the chakras with the sephirot and at the same time provide the explanations of the very prolific author, Samael Aun Weor, who thus associates the chakras and the different Churches of the Apocalypse:

Muladhara chakra   **Malkuth**   **Église d'Éphèse**

This is the starting point for all harmonization work because if the base of the building is fragile then everything else risks collapsing. It allows to channel the energies, to communicate with the elementals and also to achieve well on the physical plane.

Chakra Svadhistana   Iesod   Église de Smyrne

In this place is the link which unites the physical body to the astral body, the famous Silver cord. So by activating this chakra, astral travel will be easier, the possibility of traveling in universes, other dimensions, will be easier.

Manipura chakra   Hod et Netzach   Église de Pergame

The art of communication at all levels, with humans, spirits, the great of this world will be the gift of whoever will work to harmonize this center of energy.

Anahata chakra   Tiphereth   Église de Thyartire

Whoever opens his heart and maintains the home invites the Holy Spirit to take place there. He will be Wiser the one whose heart chakra is active and vibrates with unconditional love.

Vishuddha chakra   Guebourah et Hesed Église de Sardes

The throat chakra, as the Bible says "and the verb became flesh ", gives our speech a sacred, magical power, and also brings inspirations on the esoteric and magical level.

Ajna chakra **Binah et Hochmah** **Église de Philadelphie**

This harmonized and open chakra, with intensified work, brings the gift of clairvoyance.

Sahasrara chakra **Kether** **Église de Laodicée**

By working on this chakra one can develop the gift of reading past lives and receive pure Cosmic consciousness from the divine Mother.

In conclusion, the chakras are energy centers that run along the entire body and there are 7 main ones that are known to be found along the spine, allowing cosmic energy to flow through our subtle bodies and our physical body. These wheels of force are attached to the etheric body. They allow the energy of the Earth and that of the Cosmos to flow through the meridians. The practice of certain breathing techniques feeds these batteries with Prana.

Each of these chakras vibrates with a different color. Human beings must be seen as a microcosm within a macrocosm and in total connection with one another, consciously or not. Fear, the fears fermentation centers.

HARMONIZATION OF THE CHAKRAS

Through meditation, the recitation of mantras, the sounds of Tibetan bowls, the magic of colors, the use of certain fumigations and also the use of essential oils without forgetting the sessions of holistic medicine we can reopen these energy centers in order to harmonize them. Here comes the role of the Reiki practitioner, who, through magnetic passes on certain points of the body, will help to rebalance these chakras.

Several avenues are possible to get the chakras back into harmony.

Ayurvedic Medicine allows you to let go of bad thoughts that intoxicate the mind. Its practice is based among other things on: purification and detoxification of the body, fasting which allows us to pacify our being by balancing the 3 Doshas (vital energies: Vata, Pitta, Kapha) combined with the 5 elements; the drainage of toxins by the exercises and finally a good mental hygiene and spiritual healing by letting go, allows to let go of the bad thoughts that intoxicate the mind.

Thus Ayurvedic medicine will unite the practice of Yoga with a balanced and balanced diet supported by meditation exercises to calm the mind and allow a spiritual elevation.

The teaching of Ayurveda recognizes the principle of the 5 Elements in everything that exists in the universe. We have seen them in relation to the first 5 chakras starting from the lower Earth, Water, Fire, Air and Ether.

I recommend you the writings of Deepak Chopra which cover quite a bit this discipline which is becoming more and more known in the West.

Yoga, an ancient Indian practice, balances the physical body, the mental body and the spirit through the performance of asanas (postures) and sessions of meditation and controlled breathing. Some forms of Yoga emphasize their practice more in the recitation of mantras. The practice of Yoga allows for a healthier life, a behavior that makes a difference and often influences others through the calm and inner peace that the practitioner projects.

The effects of repeated yoga practice bring tremendous benefits such as increased energy, lower blood pressure; these practices make the heart rate more stable and lower. With the breathing techniques and the practices of asanas, the oxygen supply to the blood is increased and the blood circulation is also stimulated.

I recommend you the hatha yoga books by author Swami Sivananda who is a reference in the field.

Finally, there is the practice of Reiki, which allows the chakras to be harmonized through magnetic passes using Reiki symbols but also other symbols, esoteric, sacred or even mystical.

The benefits of the previously mentioned practices and disciplines will open up the receiver and the caregiver to universal energies that will flow more easily through their vibration centers or chakras.

There are different techniques for achieving chakra harmonization. We will see 2 of them.

Technique 1 :

The use of crystals has therapeutic virtues that help reduce physical and spiritual health problems. First of all it will be necessary to clean them, purify and charge them. One of the ways I use is to place them in the center of a pyramid by laying on of hands and fumigating with appropriate incense. After a few hours they can be removed and placed in a velvet fabric and placed in a wooden box.

We can then place the stones in the position of the 7 chakras on the bed and lie on it with a clean and light clothing. Practice the breathing techniques that are explained later and relax.

Then begin to visualize each Crystal which radiates the corresponding chakra with its energy and feel this gentle energy which penetrates your various bodies to become embedded in the Chakra in question.

The following stones can be used for the root chakra: Ruby, Garnet, Red Jasper, Agate and any other Crystal which has properties similar to those mentioned.

In the second chakra we will favor stones of orange color with the therapeutic properties corresponding to chakra 2. We will therefore use fire opal, sun stone, moon stone of course etc.

Citrine, tiger eye, yellow topaz, and other crystals will be placed under the third chakra. These crystals are mostly yellowish in color.

Below the fourth chakra we will take care to put green stones sometimes pink. We will then find jade, emerald, rose quartz, green tourmaline etc ...

For the throat chakra, stones of pale blue, sky blue such as aquamarine, blue topaz, chalcedony opal among others will be the most appropriate.

For the third eye chakra, we will use Lapis Lazuli, Azurite, Agate, blue aventurine will be good diffusers of energy to the targeted chakra.

Finally, for the crown chakra, stones with gold nuggets, or purple in color such as Amethyst, and white such as rock crystal will allow the crown chakra to be well harmonized.

After about thirty minutes lying on the stones or crystals, you can still get up calmly, without sudden movements, and go about your business. You will put the stones back in their bags and store them for later use.

Technique 2 :

Sit comfortably in your backyard, being careful to have the sun either in front of you or at its zenith. Wear loose clothing, and remove shoes or sandals so that your feet are in direct contact with the ground. Place your hands on your legs. Practice one of the breathing and relaxation methods. RELAX.

When calm is achieved physically and mentally then start by feeling that your feet are firmly on the ground and that roots are coming out to fix you to the ground. These roots go deep into the earth and multiply. These roots capture the energy of Mother Earth and bring it to your feet. Feel a gentle heat rising slowly from your toes to follow your legs, then work your way up the thighs to reach your tailbone. At this precise point, it forms a red ball which spins and amplifies. Earth energy passes through the ball to ascend to the second chakra and turns orange and forms a slowly spinning ball. The Force of planet Earth continues to rise through the orange sphere and arrives at the solar plexus chakra and takes on the yellowish tint. The power of this energy continues to follow the path of the spine and arrives at your heart chakra and becomes colored emerald green. A beautiful green sphere that vibrates with love and immense softness.

At this moment a powerful and gentle ray of the Sun issuing from the solar core penetrates the atmosphere of the earth to form a luminous and warm globe of purple color and which circles above your head.

The sunbeam continues its descent to arrive at the third eye, forming a royal blue sphere sparkling with all its splendor. The ray continues to travel to reach the throat chakra where it forms a pale blue balloon. Feel this flow of Energy continuing its descent to reach the heart where the two Solar and Telluric forces unite in a harmonious and gentle rotating movement.

Finally, you need to visualize this ball of energy at the heart chakra growing to the point where it totally engulfs you to form a shell of force around you. Stay in this position as long as possible, about ten minutes for beginners otherwise about thirty for those used to meditation.

And here you have, by these two techniques, the possibility of harmonizing your chakras, recharging them and above all protecting yourself from all harmful influences from the outside.

RECOMMENDATION

After a Chakra Harmonization session it is customary to take a warm water bath with cloves, eucalyptus leaves, and a few drops of rosemary essential oil.

The clove warms the energy center, repels negative energies and purifies the aura. This will eliminate all traces of harmful waves.

Eucalyptus strengthens vital energy and helps protection against negative energies.

Rosemary allows good recovery, attracts luck, positive waves and allows rapid purification.

So this bath then allows the recipient to complete the work of the practitioner and above all to seal the energies in him while maintaining an energy barrier repelling harmful waves.

This bath is also recommended to the practitioner who will feel the benefits.

THE DIFFERENT BODIES OF MAN

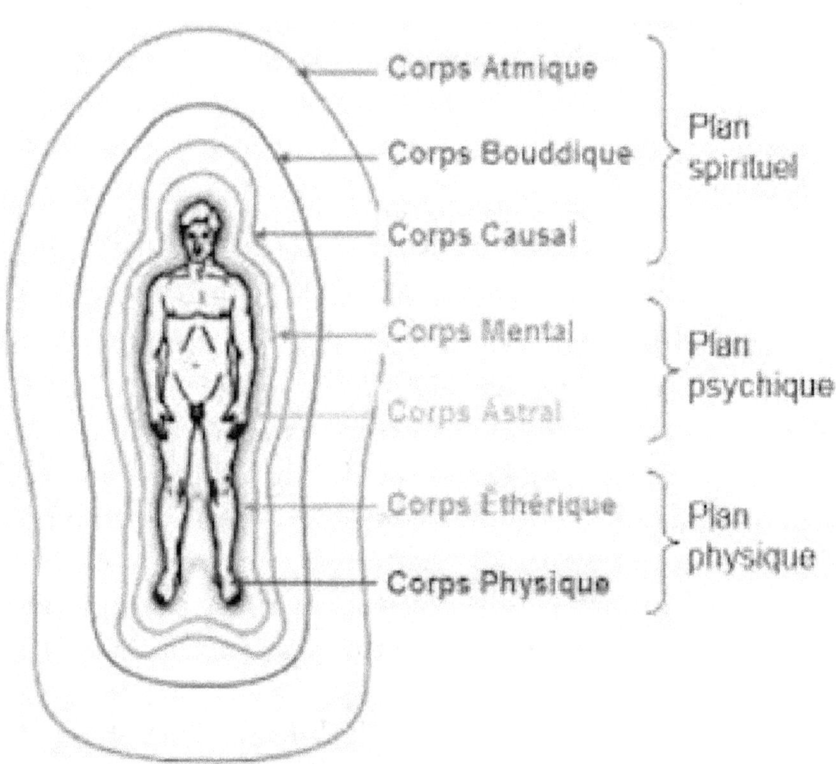

Man is made up of the Body of Soul and Spirit. According to some schools of thought man is made up of 7 bodies:

1. The physical body
2. the etheric body
3. the astral body
4. the mental body,
5. the causal body
6. The Buddhist body
7. The atmic body.

The Physical body which serves as a vehicle for the soul experiencing life on this planet. It can be thought of as an envelope with a sheet inside that is filled with character, the letter. This envelope must be kept in excellent condition in order to allow other bodies to vibrate in harmony. The root chakra is the energy center assigned to it. It is the most dense, coarse, heavy body and compared to other bodies it has a low vibration. It is advisable to work on its purification through Yoga exercises, fasting, healthy eating and meditation practices among others.

The Etheric body, also called the vital body, is the location of the energy channels called: meridians. It is the closest to the physical body, it activates the vital functions and ensures the good circulation of energies. It is also the seat of the chakras which receive, like a sensor of waves, the forces of the Cosmic to distribute them via the different channels to all the constituent bodies of the human. When you feel static current it proves that the etheric body exists. The purification of the physical body has a direct repercussion on the etheric body which is also purified.

The Astral body is the bank containing our emotions, anxieties, pains, fears but also all the feelings of well-being, joys, moments of happiness. The emotion of the moment will often be impressed on this body and can be seen through different color ranges that will tint the aura. It is this subtle body that serves as the vehicle for astral travel. When we dream or have a nightmare, it is this vehicle that travels during sleep. Some people can, by diligent practices of conscious astral travel, make an astral projection while being awake.

The Mental body is made up of:
From the higher mind which receives divine inspirations, intuitions, elavated thoughts.
From the lower mind which brings reasoning, logic, and it is influenced by ego and acquired knowledge.

This body is the box of thoughts, intellect and low consciousness. Our personality is closely linked to it. It can be influenced by our consciousness, our thoughts and also our level of spirituality.

The Causal body is the bank of our past experiences, of our previous incarnations and records the current experiences. It will be better understood that an experienced practitioner will be able to read this so-called Akashic archive and inform you about certain paths and other information that can surely help in the work of this present life.

The Buddhist body which is often in a latent state is especially developed by the Great Envoys, the Masters of Wisdom, the Servants of the divine Plan who are embodied for missions. This body allows communication with our Guardian Angels, our Instructors who work on the other side of the veil.

Finally, the Atmic body is the closest to the Divine. It is the center of Cosmic consciousness. It is at the level of the construction of this body that the cycle of incarnations ends.

Each body is united to the next and the purity of the first influences the power of the next. These bodies are planes of consciousness that reading the vibratory level of the corresponding chakra will provide information about the state of the body. Through the scan the practitioner will be able to get an idea of the state of health of the recipient's bodies.

A LITTLE PRACTICE

Relaxation is the gateway to meditation. A tense physical body makes the practice of concentration and meditation difficult. It is important to be able to allow the physical body to free itself from all muscular tension. There are several methods that can help you find this sagging muscle.

When the vehicle rolls on a flat and well-made pavement the passengers are comfortable and travel admiring the nature that passes through the windows. So it is with the different human bodies. The more relaxed the vehicle (the physical body) the more the other bodies harmonize and an inner peace is felt.

In today's world, people are often pushed to surpass themselves, to perform for the company while often forgetting themselves. We then spend more energy without the possibility of recharging quickly. With stress being constant, the circle does not stop until we shout Stop. Plan a few minutes of your time to relax and unwind. Relaxing is natural, and over-relaxing doesn't hurt. The calm that follows a relaxation session is felt in the body and the mind. We are more alert, relaxed, in a good mood in a word we are good.

You will practice progressive relaxation.
During this exercise you will need to hold each contraction for about 7 to 8 seconds. Also it is necessary to accompany the contractions by a deep breath and, by releasing the muscles, make a long and soft exhalation. Start with a comfortable posture, lie down or sit down so that your spine is aligned and no part of your body is tense. We will do this practice keeping in mind that the subject is seated. Close your eyes and feel your feet on the ground, wiggle the toes, make circular motions back and forth with the feet at ankle level about 5 times for each foot. Rest them gently on the floor and feel the muscles of the feet relaxing. Continue up to the calves and contract these muscles and release them, do this 5 times. Go up to the thighs which in turn contract and feel them free from any tension. Do the same for the gluteal muscles, abdominal muscles and pectoral muscles. Move to lower back muscles, working your way up to shoulder level. Wiggle your fingers and release all tension, twist your wrists as you would with your ankles, and place them on your thighs with palms facing up. Contract the forearm muscles followed by the biceps and triceps

and release all tension. Slowly turn your head back and forth to relax the neck muscles. Make faces and open your eyes wide, part your lips wide. Now allow calm to invade your body from head to toe through all the limbs of your body which is relaxed. Stay like this as long as possible, fifteen minutes is more than enough to start. Keep in mind that with practice driving the vehicle becomes easier and with more dexterity.

"When the breath goes astray,
The mind is unstable,
But when the breath is calm,
The mind is calm. "

Source (Hatha Yoga Pradipika)

A man can go several days without eating or drinking, but deprived of breathing, he dies within minutes. It is therefore surprising to see that this breathing so important in a man's life is little or often uncontrolled.

Breathing has two main functions: to bring more oxygen to the blood and therefore to the brain, and to control prana or life energy to achieve mastery of the mind. There are three main types of breaths: clavicular (shallow), intercostal (middle) and abdominal (deep) breathing. Full breathing combines these three phases: deep breathing that starts in the abdomen and gradually rises in the intercostal and clavicular regions. Proper breathing is done through the nose, with the mouth closed, and includes a full inhale and exhale that work all of the lungs. So breathing therefore consists of three parts in pranayama (breath control): inspiration, retention and expiration.

Breathing exercises teach you how to control prana and therefore control the mind because the two are closely related. When we are angry or afraid, our breathing is rapid and irregular; if, on the contrary, we are relaxed or in deep thought, our breathing slows down. We will do the verification by listening to the weakest sound in the room. We will see that through concentration we have unconsciously slowed down, or even held back, our breath. Since our mental state is reflected in the way we breathe, it follows that by controlling breathing we can learn to control our mental state. By breathing regularly we not only increase the amount of oxygen and prana absorbed, but we also prepare ourselves for the practice of concentration and meditation.

We'll start with basic breathing. It consists of five exercises. Kapalabhati and AnulomaViloma are the most important.

Kapalabhati :

It is one of the six purification practices in Yoga. Kapalabhati means: exercise of the shining skull and it is indeed by increasing the amount of oxygen in the body that it clears the mind and improves concentration. It consists of a series of exhale and inhale and hold breath.

The technique :

After two normal breaths, inhale then exhale while contracting the abdomen in a jerky fashion, which raises the diaphragm and completely empties the lungs; inhaling you relax the muscles to allow the lungs to fill with air. Repeat about twenty times. Then breathe in, breathe out completely, breathe in deeply, and hold the breath as long as possible without straining. Exhale slowly. The repeated movement of the diaphragm tones the stomach, heart and liver. Start with three cycles of twenty aspirations each and work your way up to sixty aspirations.

Anuloma Viloma :

In this alternating breathing exercise you inhale through one nostril, hold the breath, then exhale through the other nostril in a proportion of 4: 8: 4. The left nostril corresponds to the nadi called Ida, the right nostril to Pingala. An Anuloma Viloma cycle consists of 6 stages, explained below. Begin the practice with 10 cycles and gradually work your way up to 20, increasing the duration of each phase.

The technique :

1.- Inhale through the left nostril, closing the right with your thumb.

2.- Hold the breath by closing both nostrils

3.- Breathe out through the right nostril, keeping the ring finger and little finger on the left nostril.

4.- Inhale through the right nostril leaving the left nostril closed.

5.- Hold the breath by closing both nostrils.

6.- Breathe out through the left nostril, leaving the thumb on the right nostril.

« Thought is difficult to discover, very skillful,
running wherever it pleases.
Let the wise watch her; supervised,
it brings happiness. »

(Dhammapada, III)

During the day our mind is crossed by a quantity of positive thoughts and also negative for some. All of this affects our mood and depletes us mentally. Concentration allows us to keep our attention on a thought whatever the situation. When we let our thought wander it tends to feed on thoughts of the past or on the fears, the anxieties of the moment that pass through us. We automatically fall into a negative circle of repeating actions that are harmful to our personal development.

"Watch your thoughts, they become words.
Watch your words, they become actions.
Watch your actions, they become habits.
Watch your habits they become your character.
Watch your character, it becomes your destiny "

(Gandhi)

Indeed, the one who loses control of his thoughts risks expressing them in inappropriate words and the verb is creator. Automatically this engenders immediate or non-immediate action on the physical plane and repeats itself until the moment the harmful thought is said to be stopped. Experience shows that positive thinking is the key to success and achievement in life.

There are a variety of techniques available to help focus. Concentration on the flame of a candle or on an object is most practiced. This exercise involves staring at a candle flame without blinking for a few seconds and closing your eyes to visualize the image of that flame. You can always replace the candle with another object such as a flower, a cube, a point in the wall or any medium easy to imagine to begin with.

La technique :

In an unlit room, place a candle on a stand so that the flame is at eye level. Sit 50 to 60 centimeters away from the flame in a comfortable posture.

At first you have to stare at the base of the flame for a few minutes but at the beginning it happens that the eyes waters. It's okay, close your eyes, relax and reopen them to start over. It often happens that the gaze leaves the point of concentration, it is necessary to bring the gaze back to the base of the flame. Hold on as much as possible and close your eyes to get a mental picture of the flame or medium you choose.

Keep your eyes closed for a few minutes while holding this image. The longer you have fixed the support, the clearer the mental image will be.

This method is complete in itself. We can add a small part which consists in focusing on the breath and the bright spot of the flame. It allows to control the gaze and to be aware of the activity of the mind.

"From meditation comes wisdom."
(Bouddha)

Meditation is a practice by which one constantly observes the mind: one soothes it by concentrating it on one point in order to perceive the Self. By stopping the waves of thought, you come to understand your true nature and discover the wisdom and peace that lies within you.

For example, by concentrating on the flame of a candle, as we saw above, or on a mantra, you are constantly bringing your attention back to the object of concentration, thus reducing the movements of the mind to a small circle. . At first your thoughts will not stop wandering, but with regular practice you will be able to increase the duration of the mind's concentration.

When the attention is still unstable, meditation is called "Concentration". During this practice one holds the reins of the mind; during meditation the reins are no longer needed since the mind remains fixed on a single thought wave by itself. The one who meditates becomes one with the object of concentration because it is the ego that creates the feeling of separation or duality. With the continued practice of meditation, you will discover in yourself a greater determination and strength of will, and your mind will become clear and more focused; influencing all your actions.

As Master Swami Vishnu Devananda says: "Meditation does not come easily; a beautiful tree takes a long time to grow; you have to wait for a flower to come out, for the fruit to ripen to finally taste it. "

The flower of meditation is a peace that shines through all being. Its fruit... is indescribable.

The mind is like a lake, the surface of which is stirred by waves of thoughts. In order to see the Self that lies deep, one must first learn to calm these waves, and become the master of one's mind rather than its slave.

The two main types of meditation are: concrete or **Saguna** and abstract or **Nirguna**. In Saguna meditation, you will focus on a concrete object that the mind can easily stop at: a visual image or symbol or a mantra that will bring you to oneness. In Nirguna meditation the point of concentration is an abstract idea, like the Absolute, a concept that words cannot describe. We are going to focus on Saguna meditation.

First technique using a theme:

With your eyes closed, see yourself in the center of a square facing north. See in front of you a large brown triangle pointing up, to your left another dark blue triangle, behind you another red triangle, and finally to your right a light blue triangle. All of these triangles have their base at the edge of the square and their vertex points upward. Try to keep this image as long as possible. Now that this image is clear in your mind, connect the vertices of the triangle and form a pyramid in the center of which you will project yourself.

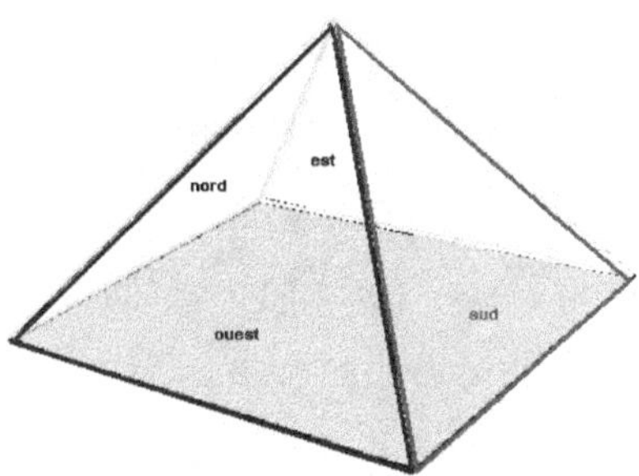

Vibrate now, being in the center of this image, the mantra: **SHYAM** (pronounced chiame) at least 8 times.

SSSSSSSSSSHHHHHHHHHHHHYYYYYYYYYYA
AAAAAAAMMMMMMMMMMM

This mantra represents cosmic love and compassion in their masculine aspect; this mantra transforms all emotions into unconditional love.

Second technique, guided meditation:

Guided meditation is simple and easy to practice. This implies that there will be at least 2 people, one of whom will lead the meditation. Before starting such a session, it will be necessary to define the method to be used and especially the subject which will serve as the central point of the meditation.

Put on some soft, relaxing music that will help calm your mind. The person conducting the meditation will go through the various techniques of relaxation, breathing and concentration. This part may take a few minutes. The guide with a soft and clear voice will invite the participants to experience the messages that she will project through visualization.

This technique is gentle and helps to develop active listening and to remain silent to achieve that inner Peace that we are looking for.

REIKI ACTION

Reiki is a discipline that unites the practitioner with the Universal Energy that flows within each of us. Some who are more sensitive feel this vibration, others perceive it by reading the aura color and the vast majority do not feel it at all.

It is certain that the practitioner is the channel but as we explained above, he must be in harmony with himself to play this role well. The Energy therefore passes through the energy centers of the therapist to pass through a laying on of hands on the recipient whose chakras will receive energy for distribution throughout the body via the nadis.

As Cosmic Energy is Life, Peace, Harmony etc ... then its field of action is great. By doing the therapy sessions, the effects will be felt by: above all a deep peace, a calm and a certain serenity. Subsequently its action will extend to the parts with the most need, this could be on a physical level or a relief or a healing of a muscle pain for example that would be accentuated. Likewise on the emotional level, calm and serenity will bring the recipient to better find himself and heal the emotional wounds engraved in his subconscious; of course without neglecting the work of the Psychologist.

The practice of Reiki helps untie the knots, how many of you have not heard of Mary who untie the knots? Blockages will be more easily mastered and canceled. Its practice greatly helps to reduce stress, to find inner peace, serenity. Imbalances will be a thing of the past, all of this of course with the work of a sincere Therapist, who knows his limits and above all who knows that all the work is the work of the Cosmic. Meditating on reiki symbols increases concentration, opens your field of consciousness and develops your sensory faculties.

The Reiki student at the first level will certainly experience the Universal Energy by: an increase in his vital force, a change in his way of life, the inner Peace which takes place little by little in him. So he will know that Reiki is working. Meditation on cosmic energy allows the student to open up more and more to become that channel through which will flow the desired blessings and graces. His harmonized chakras will vibrate at a higher frequency and blockages will give way to better flow of Energy. The more we advance in the study and the practices, the more the other bodies will take shape.

We can say without a shadow of a doubt that Reiki produces the following effects among others:

• Reiki brings back spiritual balance and mental peace;

• Reiki sweeps away energy tensions and induces complete relaxation;

• Reiki acts at all levels: mental, spiritual, physical and emotional;

• Reiki creates a balance of the energies of the various bodies;

• Reiki strengthens the body and mind at the same time;

• Reiki purifies the cells of the body;

• Reiki flows according to the patient's present needs;

• Reiki intensifies the body's natural ability to heal itself;

• Reiki can be practiced on animals and plants;

• Reiki is a holistic healing technique that is always very pleasant and gentle.

It should also be understood that the practitioner takes advantage of the wonderful effects of Reiki which pass through him to do the work on the recipient. It goes without saying that the practitioner's bodies benefit from the multiple benefits of this Energy. The master practitioner can see changes in his immediate surroundings who also benefit from the radiance of this quiet Force.

Some people ask if there is any danger in practicing reiki. Of course there is no imminent danger in its practice. However, you must always create an energy field around you that will serve as a barrier, a shield against all attacks from the opposing forces who will keep trying to get you out of the way. Indeed, whoever takes the path of spiritual awakening will be like a light shining in a park and around which a whole mass of harmful insects revolve. Your developing Energy absolutely does not please the harmful forces because you absolutely must understand that you live in this world of duality. Whoever says positive force also says negative force. An ill-intentioned practitioner could cause more damage instead of helping to resolve the recipient's problems.

The practice of the Second Chakra Harmonization Technique is also a form of protective shell creation. There are also certain prayers and mantras, decrees and affirmations that will increase the protection of the Lightworker.

TRAINING AND INITIATIONS

Becoming a Reiki Master is hard work that requires discipline, practice and diligence in the process. Reiki has 4 degrees and this training is often spread over several years. However, there is an exception to any rule. Well-born souls often take flesh to carry out missions and their contact with the Cosmic is permanent. These beings are more inclined to this kind of work and their initiation to all degrees can take place in a day, if not an hour.

Shoden : The first degree initiation, Shoden, allows for a harmonization, of the chakras, which opens the channel for the reception and transmission of energies. However, we must not hide it, the Master cannot open this channel indefinitely. This is almost untrue. Self-work is compulsory. A student who indulges in perverse practices, putting him in contact with larvae, roosters etc ... will not achieve the same results as one who leads a healthier life. A healthy mind in a healthy body is not an empty story but a course of action for any serious student who takes the path of any Initiation.

During this initiation the master teacher activates the first 2 chakras which therefore allow the student to become the channel of Cosmic Forces. Then you learn the history of Reiki of course. The teaching continues with the understanding of the 5 precepts of Reiki. The training is continuous and should not end with the teachings of the Master. This book contains all the elements necessary for a serious student who wishes to make a progress and achieve tangible results. However, the effort will always be personal and at the slightest sign of weakness you have to pull yourself together so as not to lose the gains. I encourage you to find a road partner who is also interested in the Reiki path so that one encourages the other.

This degree also teaches basic techniques of meditation, basic techniques of magnetic pass by laying on of hands accompanied by the 12 basic positions as well as methods of purification. The practice on plants, animals and on oneself and on family members should be repeated as often as possible.

Have 2 plants from the same family, for a week water both plants at the same times but run your hands over only one, being aware that you are sending this plant a fragrance of intention of harmonious development. After a few days you will see that the plant that receives this attention will be more beautiful and will develop better. It will be proof that the Love Energy you impart to this plant absolutely permeates its cells. Do the opposite to balance the energy of the one that was not developing well and see the results.

**Okuden :** The second degree begins with the study of the 3 Symbols which increase the flow of energy which, of course, flows within you; the teaching of vibrations of certain sounds and mantras that allow us to intensify our capacity as therapists to heal ourselves. More in-depth techniques of meditation and concentration will be learned to increase the vibratory rate and bring to live a deep peace. This will be accompanied by more advanced purification practices.

In the second book, we will also discuss the use of universally known symbols of certain Initiatic Orders, mandalas of certain traditions and also voodoo Vèvès.

This degree helps to achieve mental calm, calm the mind and increase the vital energy.

 **Shinpinden** : At the third degree comes the part of the spiritual journey which allows for a profound transformation. Another symbol is taught with mantras and sounds with an intense vibratory range. At this point the student is master and becomes more sensitive to the subtle vibrations. His relationship with the Universe will be more intimately. He will learn how to call upon this energy at all times by projecting himself into this ocean of Energy of Unconditional Love. He then begins to work on the ego to come to unite with the Cosmic consciously.

Some supplement with the Reiki Master Practitioner level which provides mastery of the art after years of practice and study. Certainly at this stage the Master will be able to use universally known symbols to transmit Energy to higher planes of consciousness.

The practice of silence is essential because it is in deep silence and mental calm that we receive the inspirations of the Cosmic. Also in silence we discover ourselves and any session is done in this peace which allows the receiver to find mental calm and derive the greatest benefit from it.

THE PREPARATION

Reiki sessions are always preceded by a personal purification of the practitioner. You have to cleanse your aura, your astral body, of negative energies that would cling to it during various encounters, contacts among others. This allows you to come back to begin the therapeutic practice.

Purification technique 1:

Take a glass of water and magnetize it with affirmations from the heart. Pass your hands around you, brushing your body up and down like a caress, visualizing the negative energies detaching from your various bodies. Then place your hands on the bowl of water in which you have previously placed a disc of lighted charcoal.

Then flush the water down the toilet with statements confirming that you are forever freeing yourself from these negative fluids.

Now start making the magnetic passes over your body again from bottom to top in order to bring up the energy of the Earth, where you are rooted, to the top of your head. At the end, visualize a light, of the color you feel in the moment, above the crown chakra and this light envelops you quietly to form a luminous halo all around you and voila; you are ready to start the sessions for the day.

Purification technique 2:

After your morning bath, light a charcoal disc, and take some incense that you have magnetized beforehand, and pour a small amount over the lit charcoal. Stand with your legs spread over the incense burner and let the smoke envelop you. You can recite this with confidence and feel the reach of the words in every cell of your being: May the purity of this perfume permeate my being, cleanse me of all larvae, of all negative fluids so that I become a center of force that receives and will transmit the Energy of Life, Love and Peace around me. Let it be so and it will be.

Purification technique 3:

Still waking up, standing facing the rising sun, take a deep breath. Feel the prana entering your lungs and visualize that your cells are receiving this power and becoming more and more pure. Feel your light physical body in harmony with the other bodies vibrating in harmony. Run your hands a few inches from your body up and down in quick movements with the intention of removing any harmful vibrations.

It is also necessary to practice to feel the energies of plants, animals and other people. When you arrive at a certain point you will feel the Cosmic Energy that is around and within you. At this point you will be better able to do therapy with almost absolute certainty as your faith and self-confidence will have grown through the full sensation of the vital energies.

When practicing on others, you must be sensitive to the reactions of the recipient, which will manifest in various ways:

The recipient can:

• Burst into tears

• Have a giggle

• Feel a chill, be cold

• Or any other reaction because do not forget that we are all different

Above all, do not interrupt the session because it is a sign of unlocking that is taking place. Step up passing where you were when the receiver's reactions started. It means this place needs more energy.Toute technique de connexion avec l'Énergie cosmique est recommandée. La vibration de mantras aide grandement à élever le taux vibratoire du praticien. Il est aussi recommandé d'avoir un régime de vie aussi bien qu'un régime alimentaire équilibré. La pratique du Hata Yoga aide beaucoup dans le développement de soi car cela permet de désintoxiquer le corps comme on l'avait dit dans un chapitre précédent. Enfin si vous faites partie d'un quelconque Ordre Initiatique, pratiquez les rituels, faites un avec l'Égrégore de cet Ordre qui vous sera d'une grande protection et surtout les Maîtres de l'invisible pourront vous inspirer des techniques personnelles de travail. Remerciez aussi souvent que possible le fondateur qui a légué au monde cette discipline Universelle. Il a pu, suite à une ascèse spirituelle, un détachement au monde par le jeûne et la méditation, recevoir les communications nécessaires pour arriver à transmettre ce Monument simple et puissant qu'est le Reiki.

Mikao Usui is considered an ascended master by some so we can call on his help to improve our level of knowledge of Reiki. He is available and awaits your request. This part certainly refers to your faith.

Recommendation for initiation:

After initiation the body undergoes intense transformations at all levels. For this we must help ourselves to channel the energy well. It is therefore recommended to do a period of 21 consecutive days of meditation, drink plenty of water during this period, do not consume alcohol or drugs, have a more vegetarian diet as possible and do daily self-treatment.

The 21 days is a reasonable time to allow the body to adapt to the changes but especially to start practicing self-discipline.

Meditating at least 20 minutes a day allows the mind to get used to this practice necessary for Reiki Sessions.

Water helps to physically cleanse our digestive system so that our body can properly digest breast foods and eliminate toxins ingested during unbalanced meals.

Self-treatment ensures a habit of work and also increases the vibratory rate of the different bodies, which creates a continual harmony of the Chakras. This ensures over time a mastery of the practice of Reiki.

By following these basic principles, our subconscious mind registers these positive changes that you are initiating and this increases positive attitude and determinism, eliminates nonchalance and laziness. In doing so, meditation becomes automatic and when the time to practice approaches, the body will be more arranged.

THE PRACTICE

The practice of Reiki most often begins on oneself. This requires centering and taking root. It is important to realize that we are, that we exist. There are various techniques for refocusing. Reading is one of them. Read personal development books. Read at specific times and summarize what you have read. There are also some guided meditation videos on the net that will help you a lot.

As I said, being able to feel the energy of the surrounding animals, plants, reassures and confirms that everything is energy.

Several positions of the hands on the body during the practice on oneself for a self-treatment will be learned, it is necessary to maintain these positions for 2 to 3 minutes during the treatment. The hands can be placed on the mentioned body part or just a light touch is sufficient.

I recommend reciting mantras with appropriate visualizations for self-healing. There are some esoteric currents that advocate affirmation recitation upon rising and throughout the day. These affirmations allow you to autosuggest and reprogram yourself. We become more confident and also the words are vibrations and the vibration is energy. These waves do intense work on our various bodies, creating a habit of being positive and convincing in our words. Also we have a better control of our thoughts and suddenly on the words formulated because the one who controls his words controls his actions which will surely become habits which form the character.

In conclusion, the practice is a set of techniques that allow the practitioner to better connect to cosmic energy and transfer energy by being a conscious channel of the Universal forces of Life and Truth and unconditional Love.

PRACTICAL ON SELF

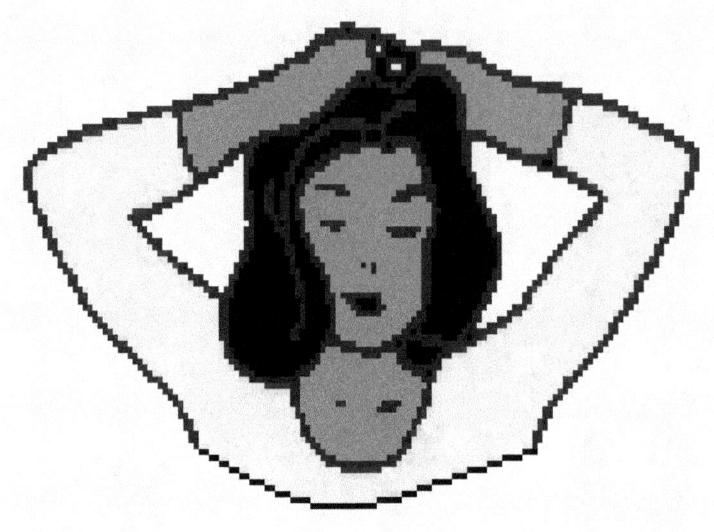

Position 1 :

Place the hands on the crown of the head about an inch from the hair. Visualize a gentle warmth coming out of your palms and entering your head; by doing this you send a flow of energy to the epiphysis which is between the two thalami. These thalami act as dispatchers. They capture external and internal information and decide where to route it and what to do with it. Likewise the Crown chakra receives information from the universe and also from you in order to route it where it is needed. By doing this practice of laying your hands on your crown chakra often, you increase your self-confidence, your intuition and most importantly your connection with the Universe.

Then put your hands in front of the eyes, feel your hands diffusing the gentle energy to your eyes which receive it and then place them on the forehead to diffuse this energy there. In doing so, we revive our mind, it helps eliminate stress and we can see our intuition heightened. The energy acts on the pituitary gland or pituitary gland, an endocrine gland that secretes a lot of hormones. If you experience headaches you can stay longer in this position so that the work can be done for personal therapy. By activating this chakra you stimulate the two hemispheres of the brain, the right where is the parasympathetic nervous system and the left seat of the sympathetic nervous system. From these practices you will begin to realize who you really are.

Position 2 :

Put your hands on the ears to relax the whole body. It also allows us to close ourselves off from the outside world and start hearing our inner voice. In Chinese medicine, the ears each have over a hundred acupuncture points. Also it is said that the ears are closely related to other organs. Often we will rub our ears like a gentle massage. For ear infections, tinnitus and balance disorders this position is suitable to provide relief.

Position 3 :

Place your hands on either side of your head, making sure your fingers are pointing upwards. It's like the two scales of a scale and it works to balance the two hemispheres of the brain. Memory is then improved and this position soothes emotional pain. This position helps to eliminate stress, helps in cases of depression without forgetting that the recipient must imperatively consult a Psychotherapist.

Position 4 :

The hands will now be placed towards the back of the head to remove fears, awaken our intuition. The mind thus finds the desired calm. You will then achieve a certain serenity. This position is in addition to the first. It stimulates the pineal and spinal gland. For cold, flu or runny nose, the position behind the head should be done. It leads to relaxation, calm and releases fear.

Position 5 :

Lower your hands as if to wrap the neck. It improves our ability to communicate and breaks down blockages. This position is recommended for singers, communicators, media people, teachers etc. If you have stiff neck problems, cervical problems and also speech difficulties (stuttering) you can stay in this position for more than 5 minutes.

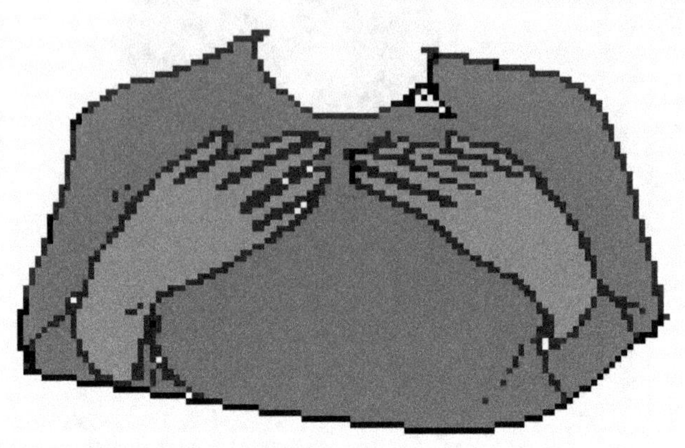

Position 6 :

Place the hands on the chest at the level of the heart to feel the joy of living, to taste the unconditional Love and also to be able to share this Love without waiting. The sixth position treats the heart, asthma, cough and lung problems. With repeated practices on this part of the body you open yourself to joy, you allow yourself to love. Also you annihilate sadness, emotional troubles are quietly eliminated.

Position 7 :

The hands then descend just below the thorax to be in front of the solar plexus. The digestive system receives energy to regulate itself and internal frustrations begin to dissipate. This is the perfect position to center yourself. The current position of the hands helps in the elimination of toxins and strengthens the liver and therefore the immune system. The energy acts on the solar plexus and helps relieve stress, anxiety and fears.

Position 8 :

The hands will be placed around the navel to further improve digestion and break down emotional blockages. This position helps treat the intestines, abdomen and regulates the digestive system. In cases of diarrhea, constipation, magnetic passes will be made on this part of the body. Emotions will then be better channeled.

Position 9 :

At the level of the pubis the hands should be placed as a descending triangle. It improves sexual abilities, strengthens your vitality, works on the bladder. Recipients such as cyclists, motorcyclists, riders are more targeted by this care at this level of the body. This chakra when receiving energy leads the recipient to stability in certain parts of his life. Work on this section of the body secures the receiver increases self-confidence and decision making.

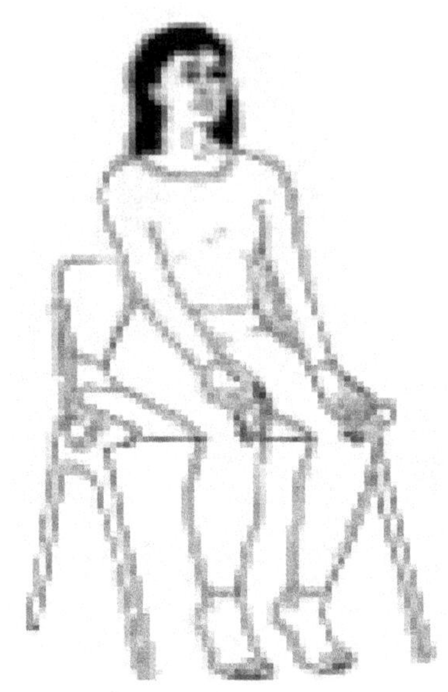

Position 10 :

Place the hands on the thighs close to the knees in order to strengthen your ability to make decisions, to get up, to stand up in difficult situations. The hands-on-thigh position calms the psyche and reduces even the fear of standing up. The decisions taken are then clearer and more certain.

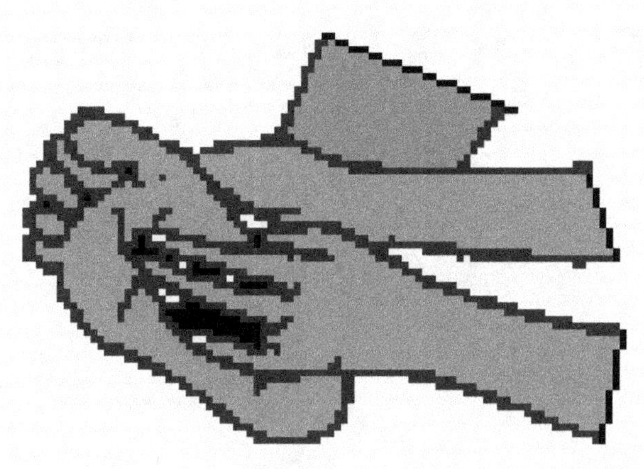

Position 11 :

Hold the feet so that the energy causes you to take root better. The invisible roots that bind you to the Earth will be stronger and more numerous and long and will penetrate deeper into the earth. It increases the energy of the body and strengthens all the organs in the body. The soles of the feet have several meridians which are closely related to the various organs of the body.

SIMPLE PRACTICE
ON OTHERS

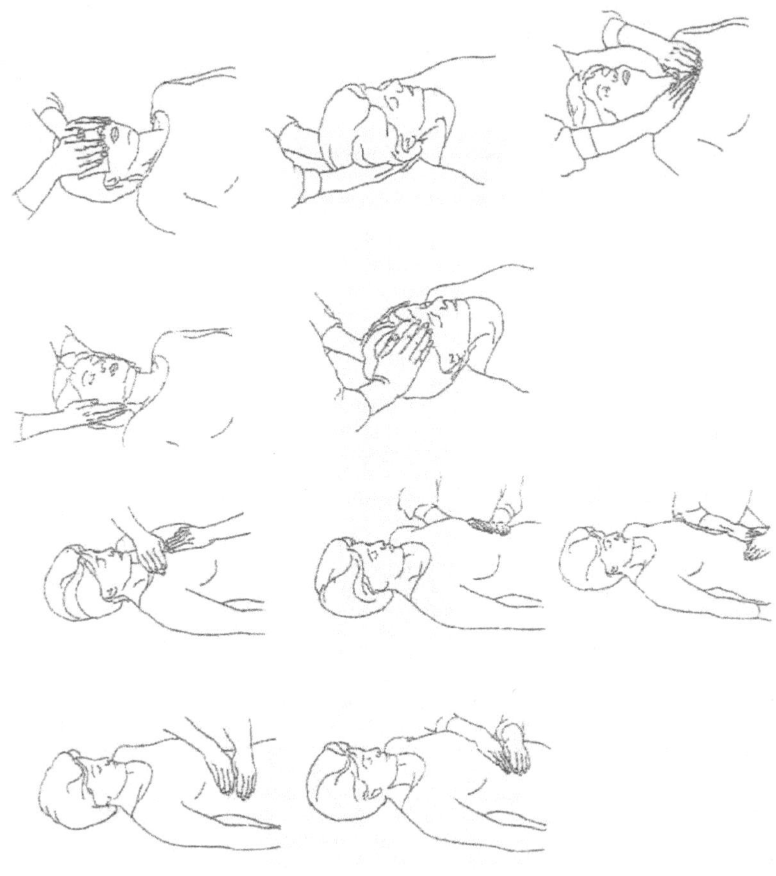

Have the person lie on their back.

The first thing to do before starting a session with others is to sit down with the person concerned and talk to them. Find out about the purpose of his approach, what drives him to come to you to benefit from Reiki treatments. It is equally important that you explain to him what Reiki is. This part is important because the first contact is a guarantee of success in the transmission of Energy or total failure. You need to let the (patient) speak freely, listen, hear any sign in their voice that might demonstrate fear, doubt, hesitation or infatuation with therapy. I say pay attention to the voice but his bodily expression will also say a lot about his mental and physical state at the time.

The person receiving the care will be lying on their back for the start of therapy sessions. Make sure you have a comfortable massage bench and also clean blankets so that the person feels good and comfortable. The room temperature should be around 68-degree Fahrenheit. You will burn incense in small quantities to create an atmosphere suitable for meditation and play soft music such as nature sounds for example. The cleanliness of the premises must be beyond reproach. The room should be welcoming and inviting.

Dimmed the light of the room so that at the end of the session, the receiver who will tend to fall asleep does not wake up and find himself dazzled by the too bright light of the room. The goal of the therapy is also to allow the beneficiary of the care to relax, to live a unique moment where he can feel free, happy, at peace and come out invigorated.

The positions presented below must be maintained for at least 3 minutes in order to allow time for the Energy to penetrate the person and become embedded in the nadis. We will stand at the level of the person's head to start the session.

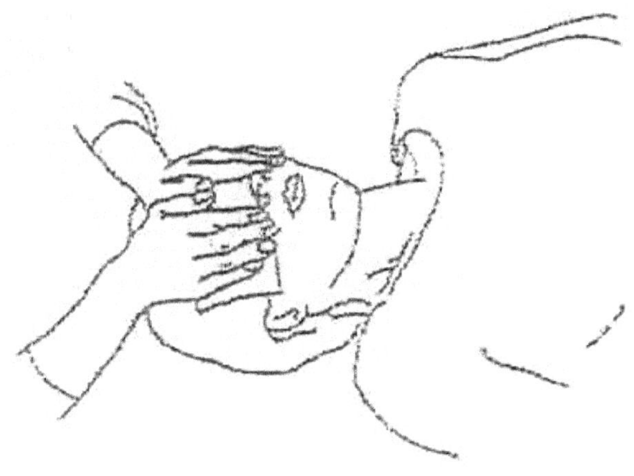

Position 1 :

Position the hands above the eyes, brushing the face. Do not cover the eyes with any fabric that will not allow the recipient to feel the warmth of your hands. This feeling is important for the one receiving the care because it will be the first tangible proof of the transfer of Energy.

It is the perfect position to bring calm, and to calm the mind. By this first position you will allow the person to develop his visualization capacities and to strengthen his intuition. The ailments that can be treated are eye problems, headaches, incessant migraines, colds and or sinusitis. You can ask Archangel Metatron to place his crown on the person's head.

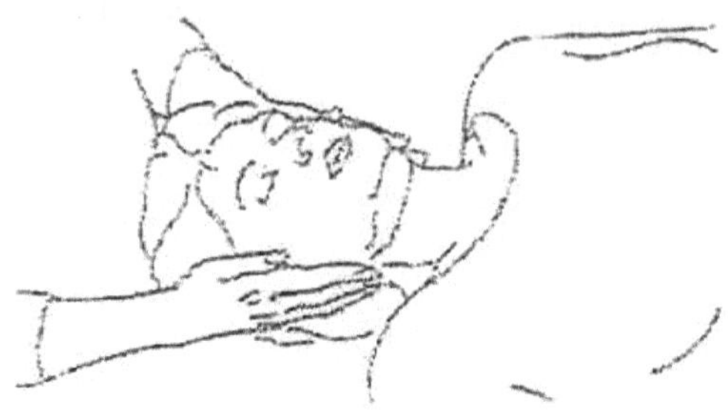

Position 2 :

Place your hands like a bowl close to each ear. In position 2 you should maintain your concentration on the balance of the brain hemispheres. This will allow the receiver to develop their intuition, to have a greater imagination, to see the rational side of things better and to have a sharper logic.

On a physical level you will hold this position in order to relieve migraines, stress and even depression in conjunction with the work of a Psychotherapist.

You must inwardly appeal to those responsible for the Sephiroth Hochmah and Binah of the tree of life for their assistance to the patient. Because these Prince

Angels have the power to help the recipient in the personal journey.

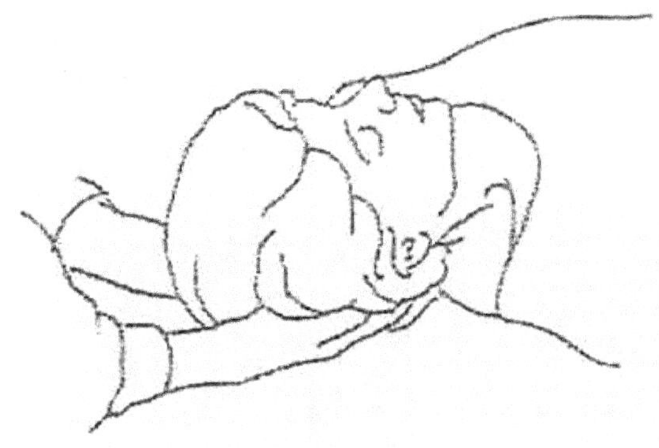

Position 3 :

Stand at the level of the person's head and place your hands under the head with the firm belief that the energy is flowing from your hands to the person's skull and brain. Always seek the help of Mikao Usui founder of reiki so that his inspiration continues to flow through you. By taking this position you complete the work started in the first position. If the person has fears, fears, have nightmares you must ask the Grand Metatron to send him his protection. You can also transmit to the person the energy of Peace, to let go which will promote their intuition. The patient will see his sleep more peaceful and longer.

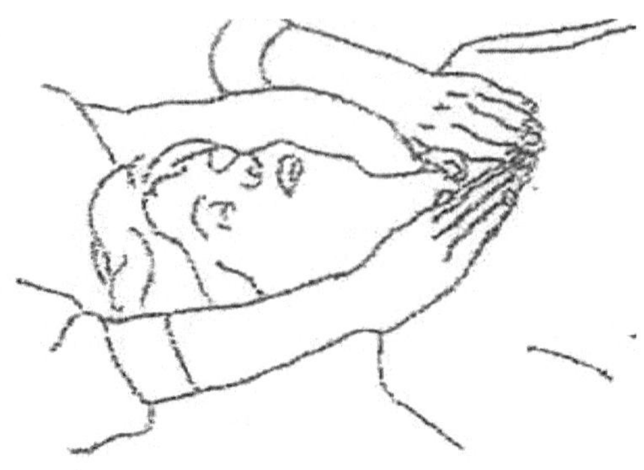

Position 4

The hands placed on the throat and neck radiate a softness that stimulates the healing of sore throats, coughs, colds and strengthens the thyroid glands. The problems of torticollis, cervical, and also the disorders of the vocal cords will be treated by this laying on of hands at this place.

In Kabbalah we often tend to associate this location with the sephirah Daat which still arouses much debate without much associated literature. Indeed, we often speak of the guardian of the threshold. Certainly the word creates then it is necessary to control this chakra in order to allow the pronunciation only of words of love, true and of peace. Call on your Guardian Angel to unite with the person's guardian angel to help them express their thoughts with clear, sweet and limpid words.

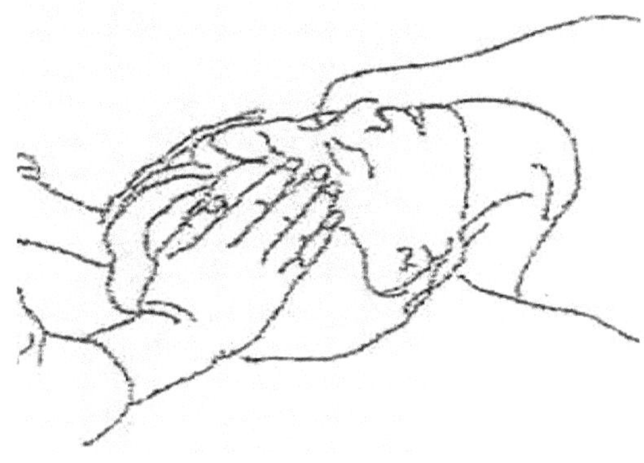

Position 5 :

This position calms the mind in a profound way and should be held with great self-control because, one should not hide it, a deviation in the control of the transfer of energy may cause more disturbance than necessary. . If you see that the person being treated has a need to develop their spirituality this is the ideal position. It is the crown of the person who activates and who will put him in contact with his inner master, his guardian and also with the Cosmic.

That being said, you should absolutely seek the help of your inner master so that the person can receive the Divine influx from the Ascended masters who are just waiting for this call. Do not hesitate to contact them before any session because their inspiration is great and sublime.

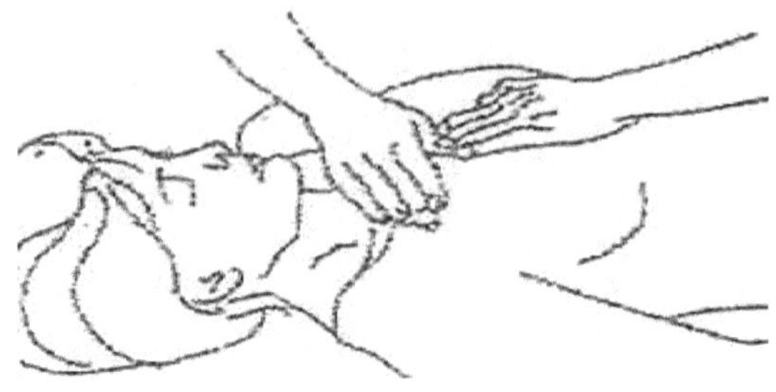

Position 6 :

The treatment of this part of the body works on pulmonary, heart, bronchitis and especially asthma problems. On a spiritual level, you will focus on fostering deep Peace, Unconditional Love in the person. Inwardly you will call the rulers of the sephiroth: Hesed and Gueburah to deposit their power of Love in the heart of the individual. You will no doubt develop emotional balance in him. You will help the person through this position to free themselves from inner fears, emotional problems that they drag along without suspecting it and especially the difficulty in loving themselves and also the fear of loving.

At this time, call for the Love of the Divine Mother, this Lady of love who transmits her boundless energy in infinite gentleness and of unique wisdom.

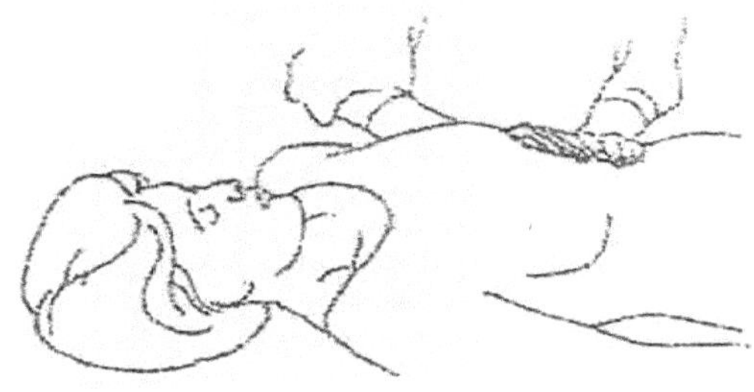

Position 7 :

You will work the left side gently to counter digestive problems, kidney stones, stomach upset too. If you find a patient fatigued, not to say physically exhausted, you need to concentrate there. People with diabetes with tendencies to hypoglycaemia will have their immune systems boosted by this affixing of the hands.

You will see in people who have disorders on this side with a lack of self-esteem, a lack of self-confidence and a fear of asserting themselves. So project your energy into power to achieve balance and subsequently eliminate these weaknesses in the person.

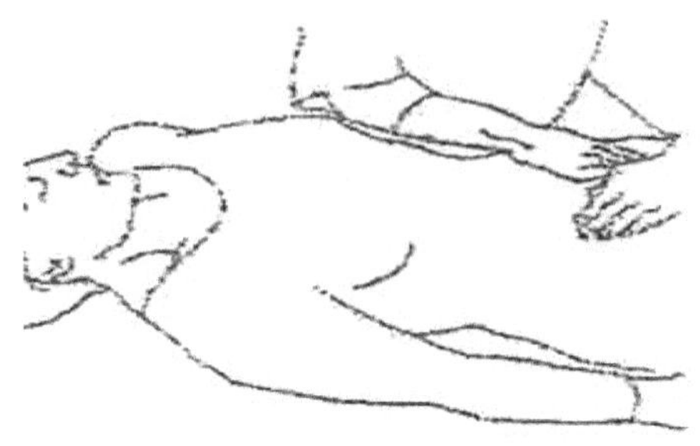

Position 8 :

You will act, by magnetizing this point, to treat constipation problems, intestinal problems, woman's difficulties during menstruation. This position allows toxins to escape from the body in a gentle and peaceful way. So call upon the ultimate divine physician, Archangel Raphael, to pour out his healing power on the organs of the sick. He will do it with love and without hesitation.

For severe depression problems, you should invite the person to see a psychotherapist first and then proceed with the laying on of hands for the transfer of the energies of comfort, inner peace, mental balance so that the individual can release all the emotions that are often blocked in this part of the body and causing the physical disorders that we have mentioned.

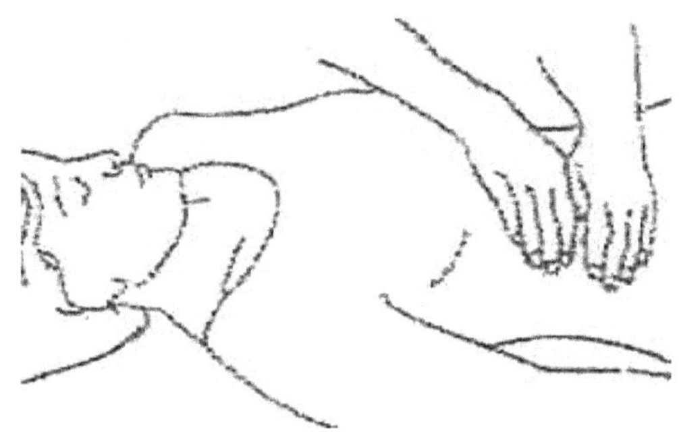

Position 9 :

This last position on the trunk will provide relief from problems with the ovaries, uterus; difficulties in procreating in men. Bladder pain will be relieved by this practice. If the woman has severe cramps during her period, difficulty ovulating or keeping the egg, then you need to spend more time magnetizing this part of the body.

You will stay in this position longer if the person is nervous, feeling anxious, or even emotionally unstable. This position will promote a clearer awareness and bring greater stability linked to a feeling of security in the person being treated.

Then turn the person onto their stomach to work the back.

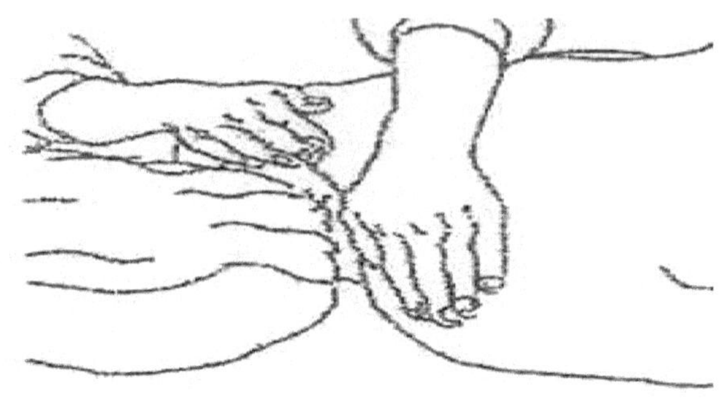

Position 1 :

The first position of the back, the hands on the shoulders, acts on the muscles of the neck and soothes pain in the cervical vertebrae. When you hold this position, you are also working on your heart, lungs etc. Often it feels like you are carrying all the problems in the world on your back. Physiologically, people who feel this way will be stiff and have severe pain in the neck.

On the emotional level, you will be able to deal with self-confidence issues and also accumulated love pains. Often people with these disorders will burst into tears. They will let out the long buried emotions. Above all, do not stop work, on the contrary, continue projecting thoughts of peace, comfort and calm to the person.

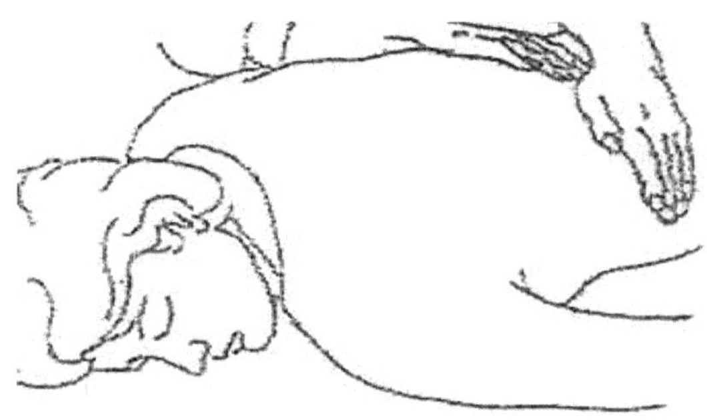

Position 2 :

In this position, you will relieve kidney problems, especially muscle tension, back pain among others. The magnetization of this place helps to strengthen the will, relieves the depressed and ensures an increase in will.

On a spiritual level, you can connect with the person's ancestors to read their past and understand some blockages so that you can better adapt the work. Open yourself up completely and let the sensations that you will receive come to you and also all the intuitions of the moment are to be considered and followed.

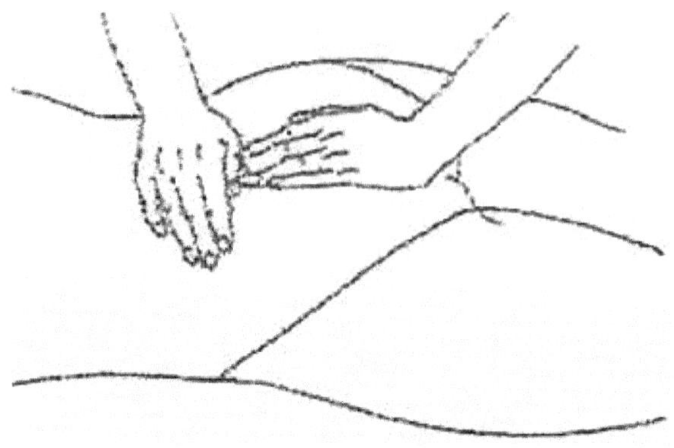

Position 3 :

This is the ideal position that you will use to provide relief from any muscle disorder, lower back problems and also diseases of organs such as intestines, kidneys, colon etc.

It is the seat of uncontrolled emotions, mental tensions and negative feelings that have haunted the person for a long time. Call on the Beings of Light to help you deal with this part deeply so that this person can stand up straight in front of everyone without fear or pent-up emotions..

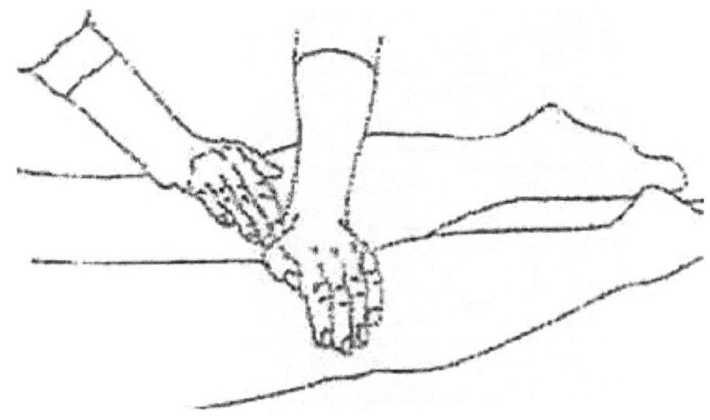

Position 4 :

Place your hands a few inches between the knees to help the person who has lost a loved one get through this moment. This position is recommended if the person suffers from a strong fear of death. If the receiver has nightmares during which he sees souls who have passed through then it is necessary to immediately appeal to the Angel of the sephirah Yesod, the Archangel Gabriel so that he brings peace of mind and also to remove in the immediate environment of this person and of his family all those souls who haunt his sleep.

For physical disorders of the knees, bladder and joint problems you will intensify your attention on this part.

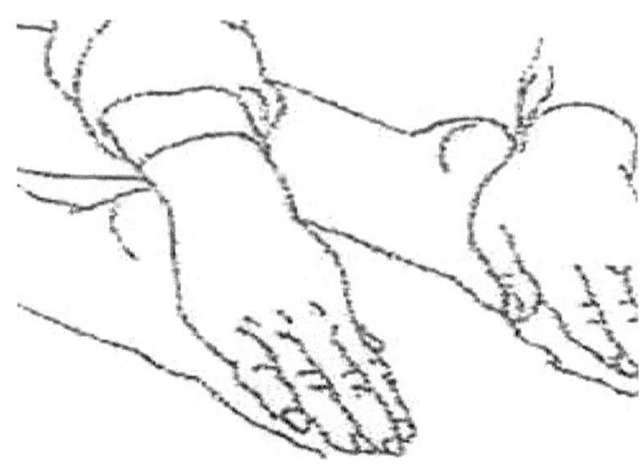

Position 5 :

Finally you will position yourself at the level of the person's feet and place your hands on them. The feet reflect all the organs of the body and by this touch you will stimulate them all. The feet are the basis of the building. A person who has difficulty asserting himself, asserting himself, standing up to assert his beliefs should receive more attention from the practitioner at this level of the body.

Call on the Angel Prince Sandalphon Regent of the Sephirah Malkuth who will know how to assist you in the work on this person.

Of course the positions are multiple, by dint of practice you will know by intuition the places where you will focus your attention during the sessions.

PROTECTION RITUALS

Working with the energies does not require any mystical, theurgic-magical knowledge, but it is also necessary to put in the head that the people on whom you will make the energy transfers will have or not been in contact with harmful forces.

Take for example a person who has dark thoughts, it is a safe bet that his etheric body is heavily filled with larvae; of lower astral entities. This person will also need spiritual and mystical help. Any flaw, any negativity has a dark force that governs them. Just as Angels inspire great qualities and the most beautiful thoughts, so perverse beings influence dark thoughts, defects, negative actions.

Is this why, the more cards we have in our sleeves, the better we will be able to cope with situations during which the patient would find himself plunged into a great depression?

In this chapter we will bring a spiritual touch to the work of the practitioner. We all use incense to scent our homes, but we sincerely know that the scent of incense brings peace, calm, serenity. This implies that the energy that the smoke from the incense gives off repels all forms of tension, all harmful miasmas in our environment. Add to this some prayers said in faith, songs that are said to be pleasing to the ears of the Angels of Peace, decrees and affirmations so we have a ritual of Divine Magic.

We are therefore going to give a fairly simple ritual that will allow you to: connect to the Cosmic, call upon Divine powers, and seal the energy in your environment.

Protection ritual:

Materials and explanation:

4 white candles or the color of the day and 4 candle holders. The lighted candle is like Aaron's rod which strikes in two places at the same time. Its flame attracts invisible energies and represents Divine light.

Grain incense: One part of myrrh, 2 parts of benzoin, one part of 3 mages. You can add powdered sage. To this mixture we will add a few drops of essential oil of Eucalyptus and Lavender.

A disc of charcoal, matches, a perfume burner (terracotta censer), a prayer book like the Sacramentary of the Rose-Croix by Robert Ambelain or the book of 24 wonderful prayers by Abbé Julio and also the Bible if you believe in it.

You will place 3 candles in the shape of a triangle, each on a candle holder, with the tip facing East and the base facing Southwest and Northwest. You will put everything you need (charcoal, censer, match, incense and prayer or mantra booklets or any inspiring book) in the middle of the invisible triangle because it is not traced. Stay a few seconds standing in the center of the triangle and take 3 deep breaths.

You will light a match saying: Fiat Lux (let there be light). Let the match burn down a bit and light the fourth candle you have in your hand saying: May the Beneficent and Creative Power of the Universe feed this candle. Imagine an intense Ray that comes from the far reaches of the universe melting into the flame of the candle in your hand.

In the middle of the triangle facing East, thank the Creator for his infinite Love, Do a mea-culpa, and ask for his assistance during this ritual of Peace and Protection. Ask him to send his Divine geniuses to you to assist you in any endeavor. Remain in meditation and feel the Sublime Presence of the Power of your Guardian Angel, of the Angels of Force, of the Heavenly Powers that the Great Creator has delegated around you to assist you.

Then light the charcoal and place it in the censer. Lay your hands on it and say: May the purifying power of the Cosmic bless this fire and make it pure.

Lay your right hand on the mixture of Incense and say: May this mixture of Frankincense and Aromatherapy be purified, blessed and consecrated to the work of the Creator.

Place the incense and the censer not too far inside the triangle.

With the first candle you lit, you will feed the others, starting with the one at Pointe East. Always with love light the candle saying: May the light of unconditional Love manifest itself in this candle here and now to shine in this room and imbue all that is there with its energy and that I can carry this Love everywhere or I'll. Let it be so and it will be.

Move to the candle you placed at the southwestern tip and light it saying: May the Power of the Motive Force of the Universe manifest here and now in this divine flame and may its radiance be felt here. and in me and is distributed by me, in me and around me. Let it be so and it will be.

Go to the third candle which was previously placed on the northwest side. Make this candle shine by saying: May My Guardian Angel be present in this candle to bring me his help and assistance in all that I have to undertake and especially during this ritual. Let it be so and it will be.

Go to the top of the triangle (eastern candle) and merge the flames of the candle in your hand with the one at the top of the triangle. Say with force: May this Triangle vibrate in all the planes of my being and in all the abode so that the Divine protection is manifest. Let it be so and it will be. At this point you can extinguish the Operator candle that you have in your hand and put it in the fourth candle holder in the center of the triangle not too far away.

Return to the center of the triangle and face East. Pour a little incense, enough not to make the smoke detector go off, saying: May the scent of this incense bless by You Lord, fill this place with its purifying energy and may the Divine Spirits who work for Evolution of Mankind be drawn by its smoke and come in Peace, Love and Harmony to Celebrate once more The Magnificence of Him who is who was and who eternally will be.

Scent the Candles starting with the Eastern one, followed by the Southwestern one and finally the Northwestern one. Return to the center of the Triangle.

Read with confidence any prayers you have chosen beforehand from one of the recommended books. Stay a few minutes in meditation with the understanding that you are protected by the Cosmic Power.

Finally say this to close the ritual: I thank you all Who assisted me during this ceremony and may Peace always be between you and me. May the Love of the Creator continue to strengthen Peace in the World.

Let it be so and it will be.

You can then exit the triangle with respect, taking care to extinguish the candles in the opposite direction that you light them.

AS A CONCLUSION

The practice of Reiki does not require becoming versed in esotericism or devotee of spirituality. However, it goes without saying that people initiates of various Initiatic Orders and those of great Spirituality will be better able to understand and apply the principles of Reiki therapy and of channeling of Energy.

Indeed, cosmic energy is universally available and we can all tap into it with love and gratitude. The work with the Cosmic brings about the development of certain faculties which are in themselves latent or already present in any Individual desiring an elevation of his state of consciousness. The Reiki Initiation will not give sacramental powers to make a rabbit appear in a hat or one to see Energy in action with a snap of the fingers. However, this initiation, supported by continuous work on oneself through meditation, concentration, the application of the 5 Reiki precepts a healthy lifestyle, will ensure a better quality of life for the practitioner and will bring him to use, for the Service of the Master Plan, the Universal Energy on

Others with a view to bringing real relief to physical or moral ailments and even at other levels.

After more than 25 years as an initiate of various Initiatic Orders, having practiced Reiki for more than 15 years, I can tell you without a doubt that the path of Spirituality is not without its difficulties. On the contrary, the path of an initiate is strewn with pitfalls of ALL KINDS. It is part of the daily bread that the famous "Our Father" Prayer speaks to us about. This daily bread is made up of the trials of life and also of the sweets that punctuate the path. This is the way the Cosmic uses to test us. So always be in gratitude willy-nilly. The universe knows what is right for you and gives it to you when you need it.

Always be honest with yourself. Learn to know and respect your limits. First of all, know that you are not a Doctor. Do not hesitate to quickly refer a person with health problems that require consultation by a health professional to a specialist for their management. Do not improvise yourself as Doctor, it willbe seen asimporter, as simple is that can be.

Do the ritual of protection often in order to build a strong barrier around you that will resist all kinds of attacks and also it will give you a habit of practicing Divine Magic rituals.

In the second Volume we will provide deeper rituals that can also be used during treatment sessions if necessary and with the patient's consent and always being careful to explain the scope of the Ritual in question.

I will end by saying with immense joy Peace in Heaven, Peace on Earth, Peace in the Entire Universe and Unconditional Love for All that exists. Thank you To the Creator who allowed me to take the time to write this book and for having inspired me with these few lines, thank you to You O Divine Mother Lady of Love, thank you to my Master Ieshouah Christos, thank you to my Guardian Angel, thank you To the protective Archangels, Thank you To the ancestral Spirits, thank you to the Ascended Masters, thank you to the Past Masters, thank you to the Great Sovereign and a special thank you to the Magnificent Goddesses who never stop loving me, inspiring me, teaching me and above all to accept me with my strengths and weaknesses.

To you who have taken the time to go through this book may the Divine Energy fill you with its Graces and may your journey be filled with inspiration and may the goal be reached while respecting your limits.

I share with you this version of the "Our Father" which was inspired in me during a meditation session:

Our Father who is in heaven, who lives in each of us and in each cell of all that exists, may your hallowed Name which encompasses all names, identify us and give us life. May your Kingdom be manifested in Us, through Us and by Us on earth in all worlds and in all kingdoms of nature. We submit to your holy and sweet will so that your Plan which is realized and will be realized in Eternity is in All the levels of our Being. Teach us to appreciated the daily bread made up of trials and also of the sweets of every moment because both are necessary for our evolution. We already know that you do not hold back our trespasses so therefore give us the strength to forgive the trespasses that are done to us because you are already forgiving, those who harm us, we, being all your children. Strengthen our Will, our Faith and our Love so that we can overcome the trials necessary for our spiritual elevation. May the spirits of evil, O Father, taste your infinite Love so that they may re-enter The Universal Source of Life and Truth that You represent. So we can say with immense joy Peace in Heaven, Peace on Earth, Peace and Infinite Love in the entire Universe.

From the Universal Church of Christ which is in
each of Us, I greet you and may the Pneuma Agion,
The Theos Pantocrator, The Divine Sophia, The
Theos Propator give you Peace, Health and make you
aware of gentleness of Unconditional Love.

Stanley Prosper to serve you.